Metaheuristics for Logistics

Metaheuristics Set

coordinated by
Nicolas Monmarché and Patrick Siarry

Volume 4

Metaheuristics for Logistics

Laurent Deroussi

WILEY

First published 2016 in Great Britain and the United States by ISTE Ltd and John Wiley & Sons, Inc.

ISTE Ltd
27-37 St George's Road
London SW19 4EU
UK

www.iste.co.uk

John Wiley & Sons, Inc.
111 River Street
Hoboken, NJ 07030
USA

www.wiley.com

Library of Congress Control Number: 2015959671

British Library Cataloguing-in-Publication Data
A CIP record for this book is available from the British Library
ISBN 978-1-84821-808-6

Contents

Introduction

General Eisenhower stated that: "*You will not find it difficult to prove that battles, campaigns, and even wars have been won or lost primarily because of logistics*". The military genius introduced the term "logistics" as the activity that allows supplying troops, temporally and spatially in order to maintain all of their operational abilities.

Logistics has progressively imposed itself in the industrial world ever since its revolution during the 19th Century, and nowadays it constitutes a means of pressure essential for the competitiveness of companies.

How can we exploit the full potential of logistics?

By bringing its flow under control and by structuring its logistic activity, which are the concerns of Supply Chain Management (SCM), several tools have been developed in various fields (manufacturing, inventory, supply and information management, etc.).

These tools can be of different kinds. They may be organizational (Lean Manufacturing, Kanban, Just-in-Time, etc.) or related to data management and use (Enterprise Resource Planning, Advanced Planning and Scheduling, Electronic Data Interchange, etc.). The scope of this work is limited to the latter category and, more specifically, to the field of decision-making tools and to the specialty they belong to, i.e. Operations Research (OR).

Robert Faure, one of the pioneers of Operations Research in France, qualified his discipline as "*the set of rational methods and techniques for the analysis and the synthesis of organizational phenomena that can be used to make better decisions*". The advent of informatics, which has revolutionized our way of thinking and allowed Operations Research to take shape, has enabled us to approach logistics from a quantitative point of view.

Logistics-related problems have been pointed out, modeled and studied. However, some of them originated in the earliest stages of logistics. They were already stimulating the minds of talented scientists in the form of numerous conundrums and other mathematical challenges that they proposed to the world.

It is all the more to these pioneers' credit that some of these problems have not been solved yet. Could it be that they are resistant to mathematics itself? Contemporary mathematicians have grouped them into two broad categories that are summarized as follows: "easy" problems and "hard" problems.

I am used to telling my students that the last person they should trust is their Operations Research professor. The words "easy" and "hard", when uttered by a professor, are quite far from their original meaning. Thus, a problem deemed easy may turn out to be tricky to solve for someone with no insider knowledge (the two-machine flow-shop scheduling problem). Likewise, a "hard" problem may seem simple at first sight (the knapsack problem). You will soon know the two problems I have given as examples inside out!

In simple terms, "easy" problems include the set of combinatorial optimization[1] problems for which we know an effective solving algorithm. This clearly shows that the number of necessary calculations is a polynomial function of the size of the problem. These problems belong to the P class of problems, which are called polynomial. On the contrary, we say that a problem is "hard" when the only algorithms we know for its solution are verified in exponential time. These problems belong to the NP class and will be called non-polynomial.

The greater part of the scientific community thinks that if we have no effective method for the solution of an NP-class problem, it is simply because there is no solution! This question, stemming from the complexity theory, is known as the "P versus NP" problem. To date, it remains unsolved and is

---

1 A combinatorial optimization problem consists of looking for the best solution among a very large, if finite, set of solutions. A more formal definition is offered in Chapter 4. All the logical problems found in this book belong to this category of problems.

classified by the Clay Mathematics Institute as one of the seven Millennium Prize Problems. A US \$1,000,000 prize will be awarded to whoever solves it.

As it happens in mathematics, whenever a problem is too complex to be solved, approximate methods are applied. Metaheuristics, which constitutes a family of generic procedures, belongs to this category. They have proved their ability to solve complex optimization problems for several years.

Throughout this book I will aim to show these procedures, to see definitively how they can be applied to logistic problems, and to understand the solutions they can provide for the quantitative optimization of the mechanism of a supply chain.

For that reason, this book is made up of 3 parts and 12 chapters.

The first part is called *"Basic Notions"*. It enables us to lay some foundations whether in relation to logistic problems or concerning optimization procedures. It includes Chapters 1 to 4.

– Chapter 1 presents us with a certain number of logistic problems in the form of exercises drawn from everyday life, which offer a first playful approach to the field. Some detailed answers, together with comments, are provided in the last chapter of this book.

– Chapter 2 draws up a methodical inventory of logistic problems, emphasizing their variety and the richness of the solutions they provide to a great number of logistic sectors. Each of these problems is presented formally in the form of a linear program. This kind of mathematical modeling, despite seeming possibly rigid, can nonetheless contain information useful for the concept of metaheuristics.

– Chapter 3 constitutes an introduction to metaheuristics. The scope of the application of these methods and the general concepts are presented. Some metaheuristic procedures are then explained in detail, while emphasis is put on their historical background, on the concepts that make them differ or bring them together, on their advantages and on their drawbacks.

– Chapter 4 constitutes a first concrete example of the application of metaheuristics. A detailed and progressive implementation, provided with comments, is proposed for an important category of optimization problems, i.e. permutation problems. This first piece of work on metaheuristics will allow us to develop a range of tools adaptable to many logistic problems and be able to give us acceptable results.

The second part is called "*Advanced notions*", as surprising as this might seem. This part aims to propose a certain number of more sophisticated tools, which will enable us to better the performance of metaheuristics. It includes Chapters 5, 6 and 7.

– The whole of Chapter 5 is dedicated to the emblematic traveling salesman problem. As for this permutation problem, metaheuristics can increase their effectiveness if they incorporate more elaborate procedures. Some of these mechanisms, such as variable neighborhood search or ejection chains, will be split into their components through the prism of the important relevant literature.

– Chapter 6 will sum up some research we have carried out in order to adapt the mechanisms mentioned in the previous chapter to the permutation flow-shop scheduling problem. This problem is also, as its name points out, a permutation problem.

– Chapter 7 aims to extend our reflection to other logistic problems that do not deal with permutation. Two general kinds of approaches are compared: the indirect approach, which consists of adapting the problem to metaheuristics and the direct approach, which consists of adapting metaheuristics to the problem.

The last part is called "*Evolutions and Current Trends*". The significance of logistic problems progressively dwindles before the current needs of the supply chain. This section is designed to define these needs and to determine the solutions that metaheuristics can provide when confronted with these new challenges. It includes Chapters 8 to 12.

– Chapter 8 introduces the concept of supply chain management. Logistic problems on their own can no longer provide satisfactory solutions to the new issues concerning the supply chain. We define the notions of horizontal and vertical synchronization in order to define the interactions between all these problems with more precision.

– Chapter 9 is also dedicated to solution methods. Faced with the study of increasingly complex systems, solving techniques have to join forces. The notion of hybridization of the optimization methods and the concept of interaction between an optimization procedure and a performance evaluation technique are studied.

– Chapter 10 describes an analysis we have carried out on flexible production systems. This study enables us to show the solutions that can be provided by an approach that combines several procedures in the study of a complex system.

– Chapter 11 describes two complex problems, set up by combining two logistic problems, which occur more and more often in the literature on the subject. These problems can clearly show the significant role they play in relation to decision-making in a supply chain. In addition to the problems, we will also describe some solving techniques present in the literature.

– Chapter 12 provides detailed solutions to the problems presented in Chapter 2.

PART 1

Basic Notions

Introductory Problems

Logistic problems are all around us. We only need to observe a little and to have some imagination to find them. In this chapter we propose three problems that perfectly illustrate the potential touch of madness of an operations researcher. These examples enable us to approach the issues that may crop up in the industrial world gradually, which will be described more formally in the following chapters. They are drawn from exam papers assigned to undergraduate students that have taken classes in a subject called "optimization problems and procedures". They are kept in their original form on purpose. The questions asked will be answered over the course of this book. A detailed answer key for the exercises, including comments, is supplied in the last chapter of this book. Beginners in combinatorial optimization can play the following little game: could you recognize the correlation between each practical problem and its theoretical equivalent?

1.1. The "swing states" problem

In the United States of America, during the presidential elections, there are certain states called "swing states", which are liable to swing from the Democratic Party towards the Republican or vice versa. It is these states that both parties pay most attention to, especially when the results day is drawing near. Table 1.1 shows the list of these states and the figures of their Electoral College.

The advisers of one of two candidates (you are free to choose either side) ask you to help them make the most of their last week of campaigning. You are also provided with, in Table 1.1, an estimate of the sum that needs to be invested in every state in order to have a chance to command a majority. There is a $500,000 global budget left to invest. The question is simple: which states should you choose in order to win the greatest number of electors?

Swing states	Electoral College	Invested sum (in K$)
North Carolina	15	80
Colorado	9	50
Florida	27	200
Indiana	11	70
Missouri	11	80
New Hampshire	4	30
New Mexico	5	50
Nevada	5	40
Ohio	20	150
Pennsylvania	21	110
Virginia	13	80
Wisconsin	10	60

Table 1.1. *List of "swing states" and estimate of the investment necessary to obtain a majority*

1) What kind of combinatorial optimization problem is the "swing state" problem in relation with?

2) Determine a criterion according to which the states can be ranked from most interesting to least interesting. Deduce a construction heuristic from this and give its principle. What solution do you find?

3) Remove the most expensive state from the last solution. Can you then complete your solution by choosing some other states, thus improving it?

4) Deduce a neighborhood system for this problem.

5) Propose the most appropriate upper and lower bounds of the optimal solution.

1.2. Adel and his camels

Your favorite Operations Research professor (we will call him Mr L.), having barely arrived in Douz[1], meets Adel, a professional camel driver. Mr L., after introducing Adel to Operations Research, works out a deal for a free excursion to the Sahara. In exchange, Mr L. has to show Adel that his knowledge in optimization can help him conduct his business more proficiently. Adel reveals to Mr L. that he has two problems. Before we tackle these, let us examine in detail our camel driver's activity.

Adel owns 12 camels. Every morning the camels need gearing up before being able to carry tourists. Two procedures are required and they have to be carried out in this order. First of all, a veterinary check-up is performed in order to make sure that the animals are in good health. Afterwards, the camels are saddled up in the Bedouin way. The time it takes to perform these two tasks varies according to the age of the animal and the kind of saddle that needs to be placed on it. These times are shown in Table 1.2. For the sake of confidentiality, we cannot tell you the names of the camels, which we will then refer to as numbers (from 1 to 12). Adel has two workers. The first one deals with the veterinary check-up. The second is an expert in Bedouin traditions and only saddles up the camels.

Camels	1	2	3	4	5	6	7	8	9	10	11	12
Veterinary check-up	10	8	12	10	14	8	4	6	16	8	6	20
Saddling-up	6	12	4	12	10	14	12	8	6	12	14	10

Table 1.2. *Time necessary to gear up the camels (in minutes)*

---

1 Douz is a small town of 17,000 people, located in the Nefzaoua region (Tunisia). If its main resource is the cultivation of the date palm, Douz is also the starting point for most camel and Méhari excursions or 4 × 4 dune rides.

1) A group of 12 tourists arrives at 10 o'clock for a camelback ride. Adel wants to fully satisfy his prestigious customers. Thus, he asks Mr L. to help him reduce their waiting time as much as possible. All the camels will have to be ready as soon as possible, given that they will start working at 8 o'clock. Mr L. offers to determine the order in which the camels will have to be geared up in order to minimize the tourists' waiting time. The problem seems so easy to him that he exults:

- What kind of optimization problem has Mr L. recognized and why does he seem so happy?

- What solving technique is Mr L. going to employ?

- What will the tourists' waiting time be?

2) On the following day, 12 other tourists arrive, but this time not all at once (see Table 1.3). Adel hopes that for every tourist that arrives, there will always be a camel ready:

- He thanks Mr L. heartily for determining the order in which the camels have to be geared up and starts calculating the sum of all the tourists' waiting times. What number will Adel find?

Tourists	A, B, C	D, E, F	G, H	I, J, K	L
Arrival time	8 : 30	9 : 00	9 : 30	10 : 00	10 : 10

Table 1.3. *Time of the tourists' arrival*

- The situation is even worse than Adel thought. The customers arriving at the same time are together, and want to set out on the ride all at once. For example, if the third camel is ready at 8:38, the three clients A, B and C (all having arrived at 8:30) will have to wait for 8 minutes, i.e. $3 \times 8 = 24$ minutes of total waiting time. What is the actual overall waiting time?

- Adel, more and more fascinated by Operations Research, then puts forward the idea that the more readily available camels should be favored. Thus, he is convinced he will find a solution that will satisfy his clients completely and sets to work. Describe and then employ a greedy heuristic procedure in relation to this idea. Will this solution satisfy Adel?

3) Adel, discouraged, turns once again to Mr L. In your opinion, how will the story end (Figure 1.1)?

Failure !

Success !

Figure 1.1. *Will Mr L. satisfy Adel's customers?*

1.3. Sauron's forges

Scary Sauron has employed you, one of his most faithful lieutenants, as his chief engineer. Your role consists of supervising the various Mordor forges and in making sure of their constant supply of iron ores so that they can produce weapons at their full capacity. Given the strategic role played by these forges in the upcoming war, there is no need to point out that your life will be inextricably linked to your productivity!

Figure 1.2 represents the map of Mordor and the locations of the different forges (numbered 1-11). The only iron mine of the whole kingdom, which is where you are located with your team and constitutes the source of supply for all the forges, is also represented on this map (as the letter M). You will also find on the map the different paths between these locations as well as the time – in hours – it takes to cover them.

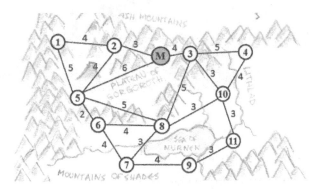

Figure 1.2. *Map of Mordor*

1.3.1. *Problem 1: The inspection of the forges*

Recently appointed, you decide to walk all over Mordor in order to supervise the set of forges:

1) Fill out the distance in Table 1.4. For each non-gray case, you will give the shortest distance from the first location (shown across the rows) to the second (shown in the columns). Why is it not necessary to provide information about every case presented in this table?

2) Your aim is to visit all the forges in Mordor. Even if you completely trust your partner (who will stand in for you at the mine during your absence), it is clear that you would like your absence to be as short as possible. Thus, you try to minimize the travel time (the time spent at the locations remaining constant). What is the name of the problem you have to solve? What solution do you obtain when you apply the "nearest neighbor" heuristic upon leaving the mine? (If several forges are equidistant, you will choose the one corresponding to the smallest number). Can you hope to obtain a better result if you apply the same technique but with a different starting point?

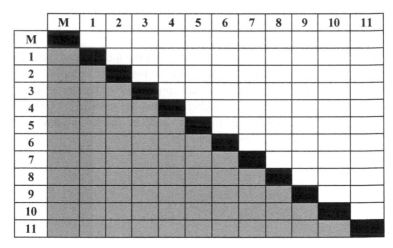

Table 1.4. *Distance between the mine and the forges*

3) Propose the best solution possible.

4) In addition to inspecting the forges, you want to carry out the delivery of iron. The volume of the iron that needs to be transported to the forges is

shown in Table 1.5. The wagon you can use to transport this load has a maximum capacity of 100 m³. Once the wagon has been loaded, its speed is reduced. So if it carries more than 75 m³, the travel time is doubled. If it transports between 50 and 75 m³, the travel time is multiplied by 1.5.

Forges	1	2	3	4	5	6	7	8	9	10	11
Volume (m³)	10	8	10	15	20	12	25	15	15	10	20

Table 1.5. *Volume (in m³) to be transported to each forge*

Without taking into account the delay on the transport time, what is this problem called? If you retrieve the best solution you found in the last part just as it is, how long will your travel time be?

Propose a division of the cities (which you will justify) into as many subsections as the number of journeys you predict to make. What solution do you find by optimizing each journey? What will be the cost of your solution? (You will propose an estimate of your solution that takes into account the context of the study. You will justify your choice).

1.3.2. *Problem 2: The production of the deadly weapon*

In the war that pits Mordor's forces against the armies of the Good, the development of new weapons plays a fundamental role. One of Sauron's generals has just built a brand new siege machine capable of smashing through the sturdiest ramparts. This enormous weapon, if produced quickly enough, could in itself turn the tide of the war and clinch the victory for your side. All the forges in the kingdom are then employed to this end. The aim is to finish the production of this weapon as soon as possible.

The machine is made up of several parts: a frame, a lever, a sling-shot, a pulley, a counterweight, three axletrees and five projectiles. Each of these parts can be produced in any forge. The production cost *units* of each of the parts is given in Table 1.6.

Parts	Frame	Lever	Sling-shot	Pulley	Counterweight	Axletree	Projectile
Production Cost	40	60	120	100	100	80	60

Table 1.6. *Production cost units for the parts of the siege machine*

Each forge has its own production capacity (or speed), which is given in Table 1.7.

So if forge 5 (with a capacity of 7 units per hour) has to produce the lever (which requires *a cost* of 60 units), it will take it 60/7 = 8.57 hours, i.e. around 9 hours (we will always round up to the next integer to take into account any possible variables during the production).

Forges	1	2	3	4	5	6	7	8	9	10	11
Capacity per hour	6	8	5	8	7	8	10	5	6	5	10

Table 1.7. *Production capacity of the forges per hour*

The machine is assembled at the mine (under your responsibility). The process can start once all the parts have arrived and it lasts 10 hours.

The time it takes to transport a part from the forge, where it has been produced to the mine, is determined thanks to the data presented in Figure 1.2. For example, the lever we have just produced will arrive at the mine in 15 hours (9 hours for the production and 6 for the transport).

The production of a part in a forge can begin straight away (at time 0). Naturally the forge needs the blueprint of the part. However, given the urgency of the task, the Nazgûls take care in person of the delivery of the blueprints (Figure 1.3), which will be carried out in a negligible amount of time.

Figure 1.3. *Nazgûl riding a winged creature*

It is definitely possible to assign the production of several parts to one forge (the number of parts that need producing is larger than the number of forges!). The production of the second part begins as soon as the first one has been completed. The three axletrees or the five projectiles can be fabricated in different forges.

Propose an empirical rule (as simple as possible) that can determine *a priori* where the parts have to be produced. By rigorously applying the rule you have set, what solution do you find? How long will it take you to produce the weapon? Propose an approach that can improve this solution.

2

A Review of Logistic Problems

After quickly presenting some historical (section 2.1) and polynomial (section 2.2) problems, we will describe over the following sections (2.3 to 2.7) some ten non-polynomial problems that represent the richness and variety of the problems we may be faced with in logistics. We will talk about packing and routing problems, production scheduling and planning, and the location of sites.

2.1. Some history

Logistics is a field that abounds with optimization problems and is, from a historical point of view, at the base of some of the best Operations Research problems. We will mention four examples that prove this point: the Fermat–Torricelli point, the Monge problem, the problem of the Seven Bridges of Königsberg and the Icosian Game.

2.1.1. *The Fermat–Torricelli point*

Pierre de Fermat formulated the following problem in 1636: "*given three points, find a fourth one such that the total distance from the three given points is the minimum possible*". The direct logistic application of this problem consists of determining the best location of a depot that should supply three cities. Popular belief is often obstinate and even today many consider the center of gravity of the triangle as the solution to this problem (is the so-called barycenter method not regularly employed to determine the location of a logistic site?). However, in 1640, Evangelista Torricelli proposed a geometrical solution to this problem (Figure 2.1). If the three angles do not exceed 120°, the Fermat-Torricelli point of a triangle actually solves Fermat's problem. This point is situated at the intersection of the concentric circles with three equilateral triangles constructed around the triangle created by the three points. If one of the angles of the triangle exceeds 120°, its vertex constitutes the point we are looking for (in this case, the Fermat–Torricelli point lies outside the triangle). This problem is a simplified form of the facility location problems described in section 2.7.

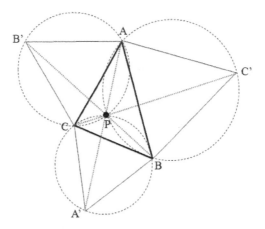

Figure 2.1. *The Fermat-Torricelli point. Point P minimizes the expression MA + MB + MC*

2.1.2. *The Monge problem*

The Monge problem is considered by some as the first Operations Research problem we have any knowledge of. It was introduced in 1781 by a French mathematician, Gaspard Monge, in his "*Mémoire sur la théorie des déblais et des remblais*". The problem consists of minimizing the transport cost for a load of dug-out earth necessary to bank a ditch. Let T be the transport function corresponding to the movement of a clod of earth from the position x towards the position $y = T(x)$ with a cost of $H(x, T(x))$. The problem consists then of minimizing the criterion $T \rightarrow \int_X H\big(x, T(x)\big)\, d\mu$

where μ is a measure that models the amount of excavated earth (Figure 2.2). The Monge problem gives birth to two well-known polynomial problems: the assignment problem (section 2.2.1) and the transportation problem (section 2.2.2).

Figure 2.2. *The Monge problem*

2.1.3. *The Seven Bridges of Königsberg and the Icosian Game*

We end this historical background with the works of Euler and Hamilton, who gave birth to what we call in graph theory "Eulerian" and "Hamiltonian" cycles, which create the basis for one of the emblematic problems of Operations Research: the traveling salesman problem (see Figure 2.3)

The Seven Bridges of Königsberg is a well-known mathematical problem. It consists of finding out whether there is a route that allows us, after starting from any area of the city (A, B, C or D), to cross each bridge only once on our way back to our starting point. Königsberg is shown schematically and as a graph on the left part of Figure 2.3. In 1736, Leonhard Euler published a document where he affirms that the problem has no solution. In graph theory, this problem is reduced to the search for a Eulerian trail (a trail that visits every edge of the graph). Such a trail exists only if all vertices in the graph have an even degree (any graph possessing this feature is called Eulerian). In the case we are considering, all vertices have an odd degree, which demonstrates that the graph is not Eulerian.

The game known as the "Icosian game" was invented in 1857 by Sir William Rowan Hamilton. The board of the game is made up of holes linked together by segments. Its representation is given on the right part of Figure 2.3. This puzzle consists of placing pieces numbered 1–20 into the holes so that two consecutive pieces, as well as pieces 1 and 20, are connected by an edge. The problem amounts to finding a "Hamiltonian cycle", i.e. a path that starts from and ends at the same point after visiting all the other points. Solving the "Icosian game" corresponds to finding a Hamiltonian cycle. In graph theory, the traveling salesman problem is formulated as the search for the shortest possible Hamiltonian cycle. Therefore, it is a problem related to the "Icosian game".

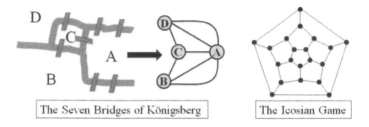

The Seven Bridges of Königsberg   The Icosian Game

Figure 2.3. *The first puzzles solved by graphs*

2.2. Some polynomial problems

There are numerous problems called polynomial that we can solve in polynomial time thanks to certain algorithms. For these problems there is then no need to employ such procedures as metaheuristics. Their significance for us will be of a completely different kind. If polynomial problems and non-polynomial problems are theoretically noticeably dissimilar, it is a different matter in practice. Sometimes it is enough to remove a certain feature from a problem to turn it into a polynomial one (or, on the contrary, to add a constraint to a polynomial problem to make it non-polynomial). There is a fine line between these two categories of problems.

Here we will only introduce those polynomial problems that will be useful at a certain stage in this book. We will leave it to the reader to discover the several other logistic polynomial problems, such as shortest path problems, maximal flow problems, the rural Chinese postman problem, etc.

2.2.1. *The assignment problem*

Let I be a set of tasks and J a set of machines. Also let $H : I \times J \to \mathbb{R}$ be a cost function that associates a cost $H(i,j) = h_{i,j}$ to each pair task-machine $(i,j) \in I \times J$. The assignment problem consists of determining the maximum matching[1] between tasks and machines and the minimal total cost.

---

1 Maximum matching means that all tasks or all machines have been matched.

In the classic assignment problem, the number of tasks is supposed to be equal to the number of machines. This problem is solved by means of the Hungarian algorithm [KUH 55]. Box 2.1 shows its mathematical formalization as an integer linear program. The objective function [2.1] minimizes the total cost of the chosen pairs. The constraints pointed out at [2.2] show that each task is assigned to exactly one machine. Similarly, the constraints defined by [2.3] show that each machine is assigned exactly one task.

Data:

$I = \{1,...,n\}, J = \{1,...,n\}$: set of n tasks and of n machines

$h_{i,j}, \forall (i,j) \in I \times J$: cost necessary to assign the task i to the machine j

Variables:

$x_{i,j} = \begin{cases} 1 \text{ if the task } i \text{ is assigned to the machine } j \\ 0 \text{ otherwise} \end{cases}, \forall (i,j) \in I \times J$

Minimize:

$$\sum_{i \in I} \sum_{j \in J} h_{i,j} \times x_{i,j} \qquad [2.1]$$

Under the constraints:

$$\sum_{j \in J} x_{i,j} = 1, \forall i \in I \qquad [2.2]$$

$$\sum_{i \in I} x_{i,j} = 1, \forall j \in J \qquad [2.3]$$

Box 2.1. *Linear program of the assignment problem*

2.2.2. *The transportation problem*

The transportation problem is a special case of the Monge problem. Let us suppose we have a set of mines I (which represent the excavated material) that have to supply raw material to a set of factories J (which represents the backfill). The transport function T from a mine $i \in I$ to a factory $j \in J$ is deemed constant. We set then a combined transport cost from the mine i to the factory j $H(i,j) = h_{i,j}$ (where $j = T(i)$). Moreover, we suppose that each mine i has an ore extraction capacity of c_i and that each factory j has a demand of d_j. The problem consists of determining the quantity of ore $q_{i,j}$ to be transported from the mines to the factories in order to satisfy the demand of the factories while respecting the capacity of the mines and minimizing the transport cost. Figure 2.4 illustrates this problem (its optimal solution, which is not hard to find, has a cost of 110 units).

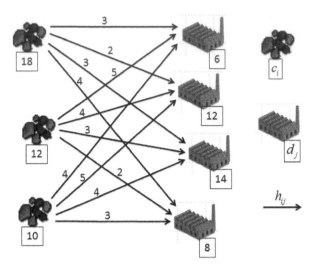

Figure 2.4. *Example of a transportation problem*

The classic problem always presupposes a state of equilibrium between supply and demand, knowing that $\sum_{i \in I} c_i = \sum_{j \in J} d_j$. If this equality is not respected, the simple fact of defining an imaginary mine or factory, with a capacity or a demand equal to $\left| \sum_{i \in I} c_i - \sum_{j \in J} d_j \right|$ and linked to the factories or to the mines with no transport costs, can lead us back to it.

Let us point out that the transportation problem is a general version of the assignment problem (with $c_i = d_j = 1$ for any i and j) and can be solved by adapting the Hungarian algorithm [MUN 57]. The mathematical model of the transportation problem is displayed in Box 2.2. The objective function [2.4] minimizes the combined transport costs. Constraints defined by [2.5] show that a mine distributes the amount of ore corresponding to its production capacity. The constraints defined by [2.6] require that the demand of the factories be satisfied.

Data:

$I = \{1,\ldots,n\}, J = \{1,\ldots,m\}$: set of n mines and of m factories

$c_i, \forall i \in I$: extraction capacity of the mines

$d_j, \forall j \in J$: demand of the factories

$h_{i,j}, \forall(i,j) \in I \times J$: combined cost of transport from mine i to factory j

Variables:

$q_{i,j} \in \mathbb{N}$ (or $\mathbb{R}^+$), $\forall(i,j) \in I \times J$: amount transported from i to j

Minimize:

$$\sum_{i \in I}\sum_{j \in J} h_{i,j} \times q_{i,j}$$ [2.4]

Under the constraints

$$\sum_{j \in J} x_{i,j} = c_i, \forall i \in I$$ [2.5]

$$\sum_{i \in I} x_{i,j} = d_j, \forall j \in J$$ [2.6]

Box 2.2. *Linear program of the transportation problem*

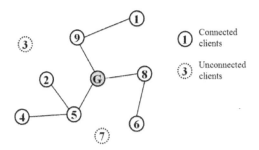

Figure 2.5. *Illustration of the Minimum-Cost Spanning Tree*

2.2.3. *The Minimum-Cost Spanning Tree problem*

Let us consider the problem shown in Figure 2.5. A generator G has to supply a set of clients (numbered 1–9). To this end, every customer has to be connected either directly to the generator (which is the case for clients 5, 8 and 9) or to another client who is already connected (as are clients 1, 2, 4 and 6). When all clients are connected (which is not the case for clients 3 and 7), the network we obtain is called a Spanning Tree in graph theory (it is formally defined as an undirected tree including all the vertices of the graph). By considering the generator as a special client, the connection between two clients i and j has a cost of $h_{i,j}$. The aim is to determine the Spanning Tree with minimal combined connection costs.

The Kruskal [KRU 56] and Prim [PRI 57] algorithms build a minimum-cost tree. A mathematical formalization is proposed in Box 2.3. The constraints pointed out at [2.8] show that whatever the division of the set I into two subsets S and $\overline{S}$, there is at least a connection between an S and an $\overline{S}$ vertex. In other words, the connectivity of the graph is guaranteed.

Data:

    $I = \{1,\ldots,n\}$: set of n vertices (including the generator)

    $h_{i,i'}, \forall (i,i') \in I \times I, i < i'$: cost of the connection between the vertices i and i'

Variables:

$$x_{i,i'} = \begin{cases} 1 \text{ if the vertices } i \text{ et } i' \text{ are connected} \\ 0 \text{ otherwise} \end{cases}, \forall (i,i') \in I \times I, i < i'$$

Minimize:

$$\sum_{i \in I} \sum_{i' \in I / i < i'} h_{i,i'} \times x_{i,i'} \qquad [2.7]$$

Under the constraints

$$\sum_{i \in S} \sum_{i' \in S} x_{\min(i,i'),\max(i,i')} \geq 1, \forall S \subset I, Card(S) \leq \left\lfloor \frac{n}{2} \right\rfloor \qquad [2.8]$$

Box 2.3. *Linear program of the Minimum-Cost Spanning Tree*

2.3. Packing problems

This list of non-polynomial logistic problems starts with the presentation of packing problems. The objective is to determine how to optimally store items in one or several receptacles (boxes, pallets, containers, trucks, etc.). We will introduce two standard problems: the knapsack problem and the bin packing problem.

2.3.1. *The knapsack problem*

This problem has the advantage of having a very simple mathematical formulation (Box 2.4), which makes it an apt example to introduce integer linear programming. We have a set of objects I. Each object I is characterized by its mass m_i and its value v_i. We have to decide which objects to carry in our knapsack, knowing that the total mass we can carry is limited by a value C, which models the capacity of the knapsack, and that we are trying to maximize the value of the objects contained in it. As for the linear program (Box 2.4), each object i is associated to a variable x_i which states whether an object is or is not contained in the knapsack. The objective function [2.9] maximizes the total value of the objects contained in the knapsack. The constraint [2.10] shows that the capacity of the knapsack is respected.

Data:

$I = \{1,\ldots,n\}$: set of n objects

$m_i, \forall i \in I$: mass of the object i

$v_i, \forall i \in I$: value of the object i

C : capacity of the knapsack

Variables:

$$x_i = \begin{cases} 1 \text{ if the object } i \text{ is in the knapsack} \\ 0 \text{ otherwise} \end{cases}, \forall i \in I$$

Maximize:

$$\sum_{i \in I} v_i x_i \qquad\qquad [2.9]$$

Under the constraints:

$$\sum_{i \in I} m_i x_i \leq C \qquad\qquad [2.10]$$

Box 2.4. *Linear program of the knapsack problem*

The knapsack problem has numerous logistic applications such as the loading of cargo, stock reservation (operational decisions) or the realization of investment plans (strategic decisions). The "swing states" example shown in the previous chapter illustrates this last point.

2.3.2. *The bin packing problem*

In its academic version (one-dimensional bin packing), the bin packing problem aims to determine the smallest number of bins, all thought to be identical, necessary to put away a set I of n objects. Each object $i \in I$ possesses a certain mass m_i. The bins have the same capacity C. In the theoretical model presented (in Box 2.5.), the number of bins is thought to be

infinite ($j \in \mathbb{N}^*$) and represents the element that needs to be minimized
[2.11]. In practice it is first necessary to determine a least upper bound that
may, for example, result from a heuristic procedure (first fit, next fit and best
fit are examples of famous heuristic procedures for this problem). Another
least upper bound, trivial and basic and yet having the advantage of being
independent from the case studied here, consists of the claim that at most we
need as many bins as there are objects to stow away, thus defining the model
by $j \in \{1,...,n\}$. This proposition is true only in the hypothesis that our
problem has a solution and thus that all the objects possess a mass smaller
than the capacity of the bins. The constraints defined by [2.12] point out is
that only the used bins j ($y_j = 1$) can contain objects, and no more than their
capacity allows. The constraints pointed out at [2.13] that each object
requires to be put away in a box.

Data:

$I = \{1,...,n\}$: set of n objects

$m_i, \forall i \in I$: mass of the object i

C : capacity of the bin

Variables:

$$x_{ij} = \begin{cases} 1 \text{ if the object } i \text{ is put in the box } j \\ 0 \text{ otherwise} \end{cases}, \forall i \in I, \forall j \in \mathbb{N}^*$$

$$y_j = \begin{cases} 1 \text{ if the box } j \text{ is used} \\ 0 \text{ otherwise} \end{cases}, \forall j \in \mathbb{N}^*$$

Minimize:

$$\sum_{j \in N} y_j \qquad\qquad [2.11]$$

Under the constraints:

$$\sum_{i \in I} m_i x_{ij} \leq C y_j, \forall j \in \mathbb{N}^* \qquad\qquad [2.12]$$

$$\qquad\qquad [2.13]$$

$$\sum_{j \in N} x_{ij} = 1, \forall i \in I$$

Box 2.5. *Linear program of the bin packing problem*

2.4. Routing problems

We present two routing problems: the traveling salesman problem and the
vehicle routing problem. These problems evidently have quite numerous

applications in supply and distribution logistics. They are also found in production logistics (minimization of machine or robot movement set-up time, etc.) or in certain very diverse fields, such as X-ray crystallography or the dating of archeological sites.

2.4.1. *The traveling salesman problem*

The TSP is certainly the most emblematic non-polynomial problem. It owes its fame, apart from its history – which makes it one of the oldest problems – to the fact that it is as easy to formulate as it is hard to solve and to its numerous applications. The TSP is formulated as follows: given a set I of n cities, in which order does a traveling salesman have to visit each of them – leaving from and returning to the same town – in order to minimize the total covered distance?

Data:

$I = \{1,...,n\}$: set of cities

$h_{i,j}, \forall(i,j) \in I \times I$: cost necessary to travel from the city i to the city j

Variables:

$$x_{i,j} = \begin{cases} 1 \text{ if the city } i \text{ precedes the city } j \\ 0 \text{ otherwise} \end{cases}, \forall(i,j) \in I \times I$$

Minimize:

$$\sum_{i \in I} \sum_{j \in I} h_{i,j} \times x_{i,j} \qquad\qquad [2.14]$$

Under the Constraints:

$$\sum_{j \in I} x_{i,j} = 1, \forall i \in I \qquad\qquad [2.15]$$

$$\sum_{i \in I} x_{i,j} = 1, \forall j \in I \qquad\qquad [2.16]$$

$$\sum_{i \in S} \sum_{j \in S} x_{i,j} \leq Card(S) - 1, \forall S \subset I, 1 \leq Card(S) \leq \left\lfloor \frac{n}{2} \right\rfloor \qquad\qquad [2.17]$$

Box 2.6. *Linear program of the TSP*

The mathematical formulation of the TSP displayed in Box 2.6 clearly shows its link with the assignment problem. The objective function [2.14], as well as the constraints pointed out at [2.15] and [2.16], are actually shared by the two kinds of problems. We are trying to allocate to each city the city that will follow according to the established route. In this model, $h_{i,j}$ represents the cost (in terms of distance) necessary to travel from the city i to the city j. By solving the assignment problem and visualizing the solutions we have obtained, we realize that there are sub-cycles (generally in large numbers). The constraints defined by [2.17], which characterize the TSP and make it a non-polynomial problem, enable us to eliminate these sub-cycles. For instance, for $S = \{1,3\}$, the corresponding constraint is written as $x_{1,3} + x_{3,1} \leq 1$ and does not allow the simultaneous presence of the two arcs (1, 3) and (3, 1) in the solution, thus preventing the presence of the sub-cycle 1-3-1.

2.4.2. The vehicle routing problem (VRP)

Let us suppose that we have $k \in K$ traveling salesmen to visit the set of cities. The problem becomes then a multiple traveling salesman problem (multiple TSP or mTSP). We introduce then a special city, which we will call the depot, where all the routes depart from and return to. The aim is to plan the route of each traveling salesman so that all cities will be visited by exactly one of them and the total distance covered by all of them will be minimal. Other criteria, such as attempting to minimize the longest route or to plan even routes, can be set.

If we also suppose that the traveling salesmen are vehicles with a capacity of $C_k, k \in K$ and that cities represent a demand $d_i, i \in I$ that needs to be satisfied, the mTSP becomes a vehicle routing problem (VRP).

In Box 2.7 we propose a mathematical model of the VRP in which the other notations are the same as those used for the TSP. As a rule, city 1 will represent the depot, which we suppose has no demand ($d_1 = 0$). The criterion that needs to be minimized [2.18] is the total distance covered by the set of vehicles. The constraint [2.19] shows that each city is served by a vehicle, whereas the depot is served by all of them. The constraints [2.20] and [2.21] show that if a vehicle serves a city, it comes from a different city and will set out to yet another. The constraints indicated at [2.22] are capacity constraints whereas the constraints pointed out at [2.23] are those concerning the elimination of sub-cycles.

2.5. Production scheduling problems

This title groups a set of problems that have important applications in the field of production management. A scheduling problem consists of determining the dates on which a set of tasks have to be carried out, given that a task needs the availability of one or several resources in order to be performed.

We show here the flow-shop and the job-shop scheduling problems, which are two kinds of shop problems. There are several other scheduling problems like, for instance, the open-shop problem, the RCPSP (Resource Constrained Project Scheduling Problem) or the HSP (Hoist Scheduling Problem).

Data:

$I = \{1,\dots,n\}$: set of cities (including the depot, which is city 1)

$K = \{1,\dots,n_k\}$: set of vehicles

$h_{i,j}, \forall(i,j) \in I \times I$: cost necessary to travel from the city i to the city j

$C_k, k \in K$: capacity of the vehicles

$d_i, i \in I$: demand of the cities

Variables:

$$x_{i,j,k} = \begin{cases} 1 \text{ if the vehicle } k \text{ travels from } i \text{ to } j \\ 0 \text{ otherwise} \end{cases}, \forall(i,j) \in I \times I, \forall k \in K$$

$$y_{i,k} = \begin{cases} 1 \text{ if the vehicle } k \text{ serves the city } i \\ 0 \text{ otherwise} \end{cases}, \forall i \in I, \forall k \in K$$

Minimize:

$$\sum_{i \in I} \sum_{j \in I} \left(h_{i,j} \times \sum_{k \in K} x_{i,j,k} \right) \tag{2.18}$$

Under the constraints:

$$\sum_{k \in K} y_{i,k} = \begin{cases} n_k \text{ if } i = 1 \\ 1 \text{ if } i = 2,\dots,n \end{cases}, \forall i \in I \tag{2.19}$$

$$\sum_{j \in I} x_{i,j,k} = y_{i,k}, \forall i \in I, \forall k \in K \tag{2.20}$$

$$\sum_{i \in I} x_{i,j,k} = y_{j,k}, \forall j \in I, \forall k \in K \tag{2.21}$$

$$\sum_{i \in I} d_i y_{i,k} \le C_k, \forall k \in K \tag{2.22}$$

$$\sum_{i \in S} \sum_{j \in S} x_{i,j,k} \le Card(S) - 1, \forall S \subset I, 1 \le Card(S) \le \left\lfloor \frac{n}{2} \right\rfloor, \forall k \in K \tag{2.23}$$

Box 2.7. *Linear program of the VRP*

2.5.1. *The flow-shop scheduling problem (FSSP)*

The flow-shop scheduling problem consists of processing a set of parts $I = \{1,\ldots,n\}$ on a set of machines $J = \{1,\ldots,m\}$, given that all parts have the same operational range, i.e. they are all processed by machine 1, then by machine 2 and so on eventually going through machine m. The machines can only process one part at a time. The processing time (or operational duration) of each part $i \in I$ in each machine $j \in J$ is written as p_{ij}. One of the usually studied objectives is the attempt to minimize the total production time for these parts, which is the difference between the entry time of the first part and the exit time of the last one. This criterion is called the makespan and is commonly noted as $C_{\max}$.

There are several versions of this problem but we will describe here the simplest one of all, which is the permutation flow-shop with a makespan criterion. The term "permutation" means that the parts cannot "overtake" one another while passing from one machine to the other, where the stocks are supposed to be handled according to a FIFO policy (first in first out).

An example with 7 parts and 3 machines are provided in Figure 2.6. We can see the matrix of the processing times as well as the Gantt chart corresponding to the permutation $\sigma = (5, 7, 4, 2, 3, 6, 1)$. The exit time (the time at which the processing in machine 3 terminates) of each part is given in the chart.

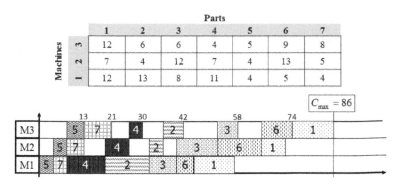

Figure 2.6. *Flow-shop scheduling problem: illustrated by an example*

The linear program of the flow-shop scheduling problem is trickier than all of those we have encountered so far. It is shown in Box 2.8. It simultaneously brings into play the decision variables $x_{i,\,k}$, which determine the position k of the part i in the permutation, and the continuous and positive variables $I_{j,\,k}$ and $W_{k,\,j}$, which represent, respectively, the idle time of the machine j between the kth and the $(k+1)^{th}$ parts and the waiting time of the kth part in the stock located between the machines j and $j+1$. The constraints [2.25] and [2.26] indicate that each part will be allocated to one position and that a position will receive one part.

Data:

$I = \{1,\ldots,n\}$: set of parts

$J = \{1,\ldots,m\}$: set of machines

$p_{i,j}, \forall(i,j) \in I \times J$: production time of the part i in the machine j

Variables:

$$x_{i,k} = \begin{cases} 1 \text{ if the part } i \text{ is located in the position } k \\ 0 \text{ otherwise} \end{cases}, \forall(i,k) \in I \times I$$

$I_{j,k} \geq 0, \forall(j,k) \in J \times I$: idle time of the machine j between the kth and $k+1^{th}$ parts.

$W_{k,j} \geq 0, \forall(k,j) \in I \times J$: waiting time of the kth part in the stock located between the machines j and $j+1$.

Minimize:

$$\sum_{j=1}^{m-1}\sum_{i=1}^{n} p_{i,j}x_{i,1} + \sum_{k=1}^{n-1} I_{m,k} \qquad [2.24]$$

Under the Constraints:

$$\sum_{i \in I} x_{i,k} = 1, \forall k \in I \qquad [2.25]$$

$$\sum_{k \in I} x_{i,k} = 1, \forall i \in I \qquad [2.26]$$

$$W_{k,j} + \sum_{i \in I} p_{i,j+1}x_{i,k} + I_{j+1,k} = I_{j,k} + \sum_{i \in I} p_{i,j}x_{i,k+1} + W_{k+1,j}$$

$$\forall k \in \{1,\ldots,n-1\}, \forall j \in \{1,\ldots,m-1\} \qquad [2.27]$$

Box 2.8. *Linear program of the FSSP*

Let us now point out the criterion that needs to be minimized [2.24] and the constraints of flow conservation [2.27]. So as to better understand this section, we introduce a transitional variable $\overline{p_{k,j}} = \sum_{i \in I} p_{i,j} x_{i,k}$ that represents the operational duration of the kth part in the machine j. According to the constraints pointed out at [2.25], for a given position k, only one of the variables $x_{i,k}$ will be equal to 1, which enables us to obtain the corresponding operational duration.

The criterion that needs to be minimized (the makespan) corresponds to the exit date of the last part (the one in the nth position) from the last machine (machine m). If we pay close attention to the performance of this machine as shown in the Gantt chart, we can see how it alternates between active and idle periods. The active periods correspond to the processing of the n parts. Their duration is then equivalent to the sum of the operational durations of the n parts in the machine m. Consequently, it is a constant value (not dependent on the processing order of the parts), which we have no need to include as element of this criterion.

Minimizing the makespan corresponds to minimizing the idle phases in the last machine. The first of these periods results from the arrival of the first part ($k = 1$), which first has to go through machines 1 to $m - 1$. This part strings along these operations with no idle time. It is easy then to determine the duration of the first idle phase $I_1 = \sum_{j=1}^{m-1} \overline{p_{1,j}} = \sum_{j=1}^{m-1} \sum_{i \in I} p_{i,j} x_{i,1}$. The other phases correspond to the inactivity of the machine m occurring in the interval between two parts and can easily be expressed by means of the sum $I_2 = \sum_{k=1}^{n-1} I_{m,k}$ thanks to the variables $I_{j,k}$. Therefore, we try to minimize the expression $I_1 + I_2$ and we find again the objective function [2.24].

The constraints pointed out at [2.27], which we called flow conservation constraints, link together all the variables. Let us focus on the interval between the end of the processing of the kth piece in the machine j and the beginning of the processing of the $(k + 1)^{th}$ piece in the machine $j +$. As Figure 2.7 shows there are two ways to measure this interval. In this picture, we define the kth piece as σ_k and we show the stock between the machines j and $j + 1$:

– The dotted line indicates the route of the kth part. Once processed by the machine j, it becomes part of the stock of the machine $j + 1$ where it remains for $W_{k,j}$ time before being handled for $P_{k,j+1}$ time. The machine $j + 1$ remains idle for $I_{j+1,k}$ time before starting to process the following task.

– The solid line considers the $(k + 1)^{th}$ part. The machine j remains idle for $I_{j, k}$ time before processing this part for $P_{k+1, j}$ time. The part becomes then part of the stock of the machine $j + 1$ where it remains for $W_{k+1, j}$ time before the next task is handled.

By showing that the difference is the same for the two routes, we obtain $W_{k,j} + \overline{p_{k,j+1}} + I_{j+1,k} = I_{j,k} + \overline{p_{k+1,j}} + W_{k+1,j}$. By replacing $\overline{p_{k,j+1}}$ and $\overline{p_{k+1,j}}$ with their respective expressions, we find exactly the constraints pointed out at [2.27].

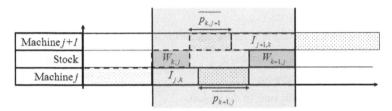

Figure 2.7.*Constraints of the flow conservation*

2.5.2. *The job-shop scheduling problem (JSSP)*

The job-shop scheduling problem is similar to the flow-shop one insofar as it always consists of processing a set of parts $I = \{1, \ldots, n\}$ on a set of machines $J = \{1, \ldots, m\}$. The difference lies in the fact that in the job-shop problem every part has its own operational range. In order to be fabricated, each part $i \in I$ requires a set of n_i operations $O_i = \{o_{i,k}, k = 1, \ldots, n_i\}$ to be carried out in a specified order (operation $o_{i,k}$ precedes operation $o_{i,k+1}$, $\forall k \in \{1, \ldots, n_i - 1\}$). Each operation $o_{i,k}$ must be performed on a machine $\mu_{i,k} \in J$ and has an operational duration of $p_{i,k}$. In Box 2.9 we propose a linear program, which draws some of its elements from the formulation put forward by [MAN 60].

The variables $x_{i, k}$ represent the time at which each task begins being processed (according to a pre-established temporal discretization). The variable t, which we minimize, represents the total process time. The constraints defined at [2.31] point out that this length of time must be greater than the time at which all parts finish being processed. Now, we only have to consider how operations can be performed on machines without overlapping and take into accounts the constraints of precedence between the operations necessary for one piece.

Data:

$I = \{1,\ldots,n\}$: set of parts

$J = \{1,\ldots,m\}$: set of machines

$O = \{o_{i,k}, i \in I, k = 1,\ldots,n_i\}$: set of operations to be processed

$(\mu_{i,k}, p_{i,k})$: machine et operational duration of the operation $o_{i,k} \in O$

Variables:

$x_{i,k} \in \mathbb{N}$: starting time for the operation $o_{i,k} \in O$

$Y_{i_1,k_1}^{i_2,k_2} = \begin{cases} 1 \text{ if } o_{i_1,k_1} \text{ precedes } o_{i_2,k_2} \\ 0 \text{ otherwise} \end{cases}$, $\forall (o_{i_1,k_1}, o_{i_2,k_2}) \in O \times O, \mu_{i_1,k_1} = \mu_{i_2,k_2}$

$t \in \mathbb{N}$: finishing time of the project

Minimize: t

Under the constraints:

$(M + p_{i_1,k_1}) Y_{i_1,k_1}^{i_2,k_2} + (x_{i_1,k_1} - x_{i_2,k_2}) \geq p_{i_2,k_2}$, $\forall (o_{i_1,k_1}, o_{i_2,k_2}) \in O^2, \mu_{i_1,k_1} = \mu_{i_2,k_2}$ [2.28]

$(M + p_{i_2,k_2})(1 - Y_{i_1,k_1}^{i_2,k_2}) + (x_{i_2,k_2} - x_{i_1,k_1}) \geq p_{i_1,k_1}$ $\forall (o_{i_1,k_1}, o_{i_2,k_2}) \in O^2, \mu_{i_1,k_1} = \mu_{i_2,k_2}$ [2.29]

$x_{i,j+1} \geq x_{i,j} + p_{i,j}$, $\forall i \in I, k \in \{1,\ldots,n_i - 1\}$ [2.30]

$x_{i,n_i} + p_{i,n_i} \leq t$, $\forall i \in I$ [2.31]

Box 2.9. *Linear program of the JSSP*

Precedence constraints are simply defined by means of the constraints pointed out at [2.30], which require that, for the same part, an operation has to be carried out before the next one can start.

Non-overlap constraints are less evident. We know perfectly well the set of operations that each machine $j \in J$ has to perform. Let o_{i_1,k_1} and o_{i_2,k_2} be two operations performed on the same machine j ($\mu_{i_1,k_1} = \mu_{i_2,k_2} = j$). These constraints imply that $x_{i_2,k_2} + p_{i_2,k_2} \leq x_{i_1,k_1}$ (the operation o_{i_1,k_1} cannot start until the operation o_{i_2,k_2} has terminated) or that $x_{i_1,k_1} + p_{i_1,k_1} \leq x_{i_2,k_2}$ (the operation o_{i_2,k_2} cannot start until the operation o_{i_1,k_1} has terminated). To linearize the logical operator "or", decision variables $Y_{i_1,k_1}^{i_2,k_2}$ are introduced for each pair of operations that need to be processed on the same machine. Non-overlap constraints are expressed by constraints [2.28] and [2.29], where M represents an arbitrarily large value (any upper bound of the project duration is suitable). They work as follows. If $Y_{i_1,k_1}^{i_2,k_2} = 1$ (respectively $Y_{i_1,k_1}^{i_2,k_2} = 0$) then the constraint [2.29] (respectively [2.28]) requires that $x_{i_2,k_2} - x_{i_1,k_1} \geq p_{i_1,k_1}$ (respectively $x_{i_1,k_1} - x_{i_2,k_2} \geq p_{i_2,k_2}$), so that $x_{i_1,k_1} + p_{i_1,k_1} \leq x_{i_2,k_2}$ (respectively $x_{i_2,k_2} + p_{i_2,k_2} \leq x_{i_1,k_1}$). The other constraint is always satisfied.

2.6. Lot-sizing problems

Production planning and assignment are both contained within the larger framework of production management. Here, we focus more specifically on those problems that try to determine which and how many products will be produced in any given period. The planning horizon generally lasts several months with weekly time frames. These kinds of problems, called lot-sizing problems in the scientific literature, are on the one hand based on firm commands and on the other on predictions, and mainly have to do with the development of the Master Production Schedule (MPS). There are several models. We advise the reader to consult [DRE 97], who reviews the latest developments of the principal lot-sizing problems in comprehensible terms. We propose here the CLSP (Capacitated Lot-Sizing Problem), which is one of the basic problems of this category. We point out straight away that if our fill rate is infinite (which amounts to removing capacity constraints), the CLSP model turns into the Wagner–Whitin model, which is a polynomial problem [WAG 58].

The CLSP consists of planning the production of a set of products I over a time horizon T, artificially divided up into time frames. The aim is to satisfy the demand $d_{i,t}$ (which is supposed to be known, whether it is stable or partially estimated) for each product $i \in I$ in every phase $t \in T$, while keeping within the bounds of the production capacity and minimizing the costs. In every phase t we have available a production capacity C_t, knowing that the production of a product unit i requires a part p_i of this capacity. The costs we take into account for this model are the product introduction s_i and holding h_i costs over a period of time. It is a matter of mediating between these two conflicting kinds of costs. Economizing on the introduction cost will entail a larger production and consequently a stock build-up. The last piece of information provided by the formulation of the problem tells us that the initial stock value $S_{i,0}$ of each product is known.

The CLSP can be formulated as a mixed linear program (Box 2.10). The variables used for this model are $X_{i,t} \geq 0$, which represents the amount of product i to be manufactured in a period of time t, $Y_{i,t} \in \{0,1\}$, which determines the necessary product launches, and $S_{i,t} \geq 0$, which shows the stock levels.

The function that needs to be minimized is the sum of the introduction and holding costs [2.32]. The constraints pointed out at [2.33] ensure stock stability. For every product, the stock at any given time is equal to the stock of the preceding period plus the amount produced in the current period minus the demand. The constraints pointed out at [2.34] compel a product to be launched once it has been manufactured in a period of time. Finally, the constraints expressed by [2.34] are capacity constraints.

Data:

T : set of periods

I : set of products

$d_{i,t}, \forall i \in I, \forall t \in T$: demand of the product i in the period t

$h_i, \forall i \in I$: holding cost of a product unit i

$S_{i,0}, \forall i \in I$: initial stock of the product i

$s_i, \forall i \in I$: introduction cost of the product i

$p_i, \forall i \in I$: capacity required to manufacture a product unit i

$C_t, \forall t \in T$: production capacity for a period t

Variables:

$X_{i,t} \geq 0, \forall (i,t) \in I \times T$: amount of products i manufactured in the period t

$Y_{i,t} = \begin{cases} 1 \text{ if the product } i \text{ is manufactured during the period } t \\ 0 \text{ otherwise} \end{cases}, \forall (i,t) \in I \times T,$

$S_{i,t}, \forall (i,t) \in I \times T$: stock level of the product i in the period t

Minimize $\sum_{t \in T} \sum_{i \in I} \left(s_i Y_{i,t} + h_i S_{i,t} \right)$ [2.32]

Under the constraints

$S_{i,t} = S_{i,t-1} + X_{i,t} - d_{i,t}, \forall (i,t) \in I \times T$ [2.33]

$p_i X_{i,t} \leq C_t Y_{i,t}, \forall i \in I$ [2.34]

$\sum_{i \in I} p_i X_{i,t} \leq C_t, \forall t \in T$ [2.35]

Box 2.10. *Linear program of the CLSP*

2.7. Facility location problems

We conclude this catalog of logistic problems with facility location problems, which aim to determine the optimal placement of facilities (whether they are production, stock or distribution facilities, etc) in order to minimize the combined cost. These problems are designed to set up the most effective supply chain. We will show two models: a static one – the Uncapacitated Plant Location Problem (UPLP) – and a dynamic one – the Dynamic Location Problem. A model is said to be dynamic if, when working with periods of time, it allows the supply chain to evolve over time.

2.7.1. *The Uncapacitated Plant Location Problem (UPLP)*

Fermat's problem, which we presented at the beginning of this chapter, consists of finding a location for a facility in order to supply three clients. The UPLP is its generalized version with an n number of locations and clients.

The formulation of the problem is as follows. We have a set of potential locations I that can accommodate facilities. Setting up a facility on a location $i \in I$ entails a cost of o_i. The facilities have to supply a set of clients J. More precisely, each client must be supplied by only one facility and will then be allocated to it. $tr_{i,j}$ represents the cost of the distribution between the location i and the client j. The problem consists of determining the locations at which facilities should be set up and which clients should be supplied by these facilities in order to minimize the total cost of the set-up and of the distribution.

The linear program (Box 2.11) of the UPLP employs the variables $X_{i,j} \in \{0,1\}$, which shows whether the site i supplies the client j, and $Y_i \in \{0,1\}$, which indicates whether a facility i has been set up or not. The objective function [2.36] minimizes the sum of the costs. The first term of the sum represents the set-up costs whereas the second one represents the distribution costs. The constraints pointed out at [2.37] assign each client to a facility. The constraints defined by [2.38] indicate that only the facilities that have been set up can supply clients, having, however, no restriction in relation to the number of clients they can supply.

Data:

> I : set of potential locations for the setting up
> J : set of clients that need to be supplied
> $D_j, \forall j \in J$: demand of the client j
> $C_i, \forall i \in I$: capacity of the facility i
> $o_i, \forall i \in I$: setting-up cost of the facility i
> $tr_{i,j}, \forall (i,j) \in I \times J$: Transport cost of a unit from the facility i to the client j

Variables:

$$X_{i,j} = \begin{cases} 1 \text{ if the facility } i \text{ supplies the client } j, \forall (i,j) \in I \times J \\ 0 \text{ otherwise} \end{cases}$$

$$Y_i = \begin{cases} 1 \text{ if the facility } i \text{ is open }, \forall i \in I \\ 0 \text{ otherwise} \end{cases},$$

Minimize: $\sum_{i \in I} o_i Y_i + \sum_{i \in I} \sum_{j \in J} tr_{i,j} X_{i,j}$ [2.36]

Under the constraints:

$$\sum_{i \in I} X_{i,j} = 1, \forall j \in J \qquad [2.37]$$

$$\sum_{j \in J} X_{i,j} \le Card(J) \times Y_i, \forall i \in I \qquad [2.38]$$

Box 2.11. *Linear program of the UPLP*

The CPLP (Capacitated Plant Location Problem) is an important version of the UPLP that includes capacity constraints. Each facility $i \in I$ has a capacity C_i and each client $j \in J$ has a demand d_j that needs to be met. It is enough then to replace the constraints defined by [2.38] with those pointed out in [2.38a]:

$$\sum_{j \in J} d_j X_{i,j} \le C_i Y_i, \forall i \in I \qquad [2.38a]$$

A second variant we often find is the k-median. The number of facilities that need to be set up is established beforehand as a value k. It is enough to add the constraint defined by [2.38b] to the UPLP:

$$\sum_{i \in I} Y_i = k \qquad [2.38b]$$

2.7.2. *The Dynamic Location Problem (DLP)*

The Dynamic Location Problem (DLP), by working on a time horizon is divided into time frames, allowing the logistic network to evolve over time by opening or closing structures. New issues can thus be considered: should we open or close facilities? If so, then "which ones?"; "when was it?"; "is it suitable to increase or reduce the capacity of a facility?"; and so on.

Data:

$I = I_o \cup I_c$: set of open and closed facilities

J : set of clients that need to be supplied

$T = \{1,\ldots,NT\}$: set of NT periods

$o_{i,t}$, $\forall (i,t) \in I \times T$: cost necessary to exploit the facility i during the period t

$tr_{i,j,t}$, $\forall (i,j,t) \in I \times J \times T$: transport cost for a unit i to j during the period t

Variables:

$$X_{i,j,t} = \begin{cases} 1 \text{ if the facility } i \text{ supplies the client } j \text{ during the period } t \text{ ,} \\ 0 \text{ otherwise} \end{cases}$$

$$\forall (i,j,t) \in I \times J \times T$$

$$Y_{i,t} = \begin{cases} 1 \text{ if the facility } i \text{ is open during the period } t \text{ , } \forall (i,t) \in I \times T \\ 0 \text{ otherwise} \end{cases},$$

Minimize: $\sum_{t\in T}\sum_{i\in I} o_{i,t} Y_{i,t} + \sum_{t\in T}\sum_{i\in I}\sum_{j\in J} tr_{i,j,t} X_{i,j,t}$ [2.39]

Under the constraints:

$$\sum_{i\in I} X_{i,j,t} = 1, \forall (j,t) \in J \times T$$ [2.40]

$$\sum_{j\in J} X_{i,j,t} \leq Card(J) \times Y_{i,t}, \forall (i,t) \in I \times T$$ [2.41]

$$Y_{i,t} \geq Y_{i,t+1}, \forall i \in I_c, \forall t \in T \setminus \{NT\}$$ [2.42]

$$Y_{i,t} \leq Y_{i,t+1}, \forall i \in I_o, \forall t \in T \setminus \{NT\}$$ [2.43]

Box 2.12. *Linear program of the DLP*

The model shown here (Box 2.12) is drawn from [DAG 98]. It consists of an extension of the UPLP, which includes periods of time. Thus, most data and variables are indexed on the time frames. This is the case for the clients' demand, the capacity of the facilities, the transport or set-up costs, and makes it possible to take into account predictions of economic development in the model. The most significant difference lies in the addition of the following hypothesis. It will no longer be possible to close a facility that opens at a given time. Likewise, it will be impossible to re-open a facility that shuts down. These hypotheses represent how opening or closing a facility is an important decision that cannot be reconsidered over the time considered.

Another significant difference between the two models lies in the fact that the UPLP is designed to envisage the logistic network, whereas the DLP attempts to make it evolve. So, the last model relies on a logistic network present at the beginning of this study. For that reason I is divided up into two subsets: I_o, which represents the set of locations where a new factory can be set up, and I_c, which groups together the existing facilities that may shut down.

The objective function [2.39] and the constraints [2.40] and [2.41] resemble those of the UPLP. The constraints pointed out in [2.42] require the variables $Y_{i,t}$ to form a decreasing sequence for the existing facilities. These can only shut down over the time horizon. The constraints defined by [2.44] state that variables $Y_{i,t}$ have to form an increasing sequence for the potential facilities, which can only open over the time horizon.

2.8. Conclusion

Throughout the chapter we had the opportunity to catalog several theoretical problems that may crop up as often in different logistic activities (supply, production, stock and distribution) as they do on any kind of decisional level. The problems described here are both numerous and diverse. However, they share the fact that they all belong to that category of problems called non-polynomial. Thus, they quickly become quite complex, if not impossible, to solve with the classic ILP techniques.

To make things worse, the actual problems with which companies are faced generally involve quite substantial sizes and can include specific location constraints, which may turn out to be tricky, if only to model linearly.

Metaheuristics are solving techniques that can provide solutions to all the points we have just brought up. The next chapter will be dedicated to their analysis.

3

An Introduction to Metaheuristics

As we saw throughout the last two chapters, by attempting to optimize the workings of a supply chain, we will have the opportunity to deal with quite a few problems that crop up at different stages in the chain or at different points in the time horizon (short-term, medium-term, or long-term). The term "*optimize*", behind which lie numerous logistic issues, is here meant in its mathematical sense. Each solution is assessed quantitatively by means of a function called objective, so that any two solutions can be compared. Optimizing the supply chain consists then in finding the best solution in relation to the objective we have thus defined. Metaheuristics are optimization techniques that are quite suitable as solving aids for logistic problems. First we will endeavor to give a definition of metaheuristics and to define the scope of their applications. Then we will deal with local search before introducing some metaheuristic procedures by separating individual-based methods from population-based ones.

3.1. Optimization problems

Generally an optimization problem can be defined as the problem of finding a solution X^* in a domain S that optimizes a function H often called cost function or objective function. More formally, let $X = (x_1, x_2, \ldots, x_n)$ be a vector made up of n real or integer variables, S the set of feasible solutions – i.e. verifying the set of constraints of the problem – and $H : S \rightarrow \mathbb{R}$ the objective function. An optimization problem consists of solving $opt_{X \in S} \{H(X)\}$, where opt represents a minimization or a maximization problem. The set of optimal solutions is written as S^*.

An optimization problem is first characterized by the nature of its variables. Thus, it is said to be continuous when all variables are real, discrete or combinatorial when there are only integer variables, and mixed when it combines both kinds.

Then an optimization problem is defined by the nature of its constraints and of its objective variable. A problem is said to be linear if all of its constraints and its objective function are described linearly and as non-linear when they are not.

The most classic mathematical techniques used to solve continuous optimization problems are based on the gradient algorithm (Box 3.1). These techniques, which date back to the 19th Century, are employed to optimize an objective function differentiable in a Euclidean space, for example a part of $\mathbb{R}^n$.

$Gradient\ function(x_0, \varepsilon)$

      Initialize $x \leftarrow x_0$

      Calculate $\nabla H(x)$

      While $\left\|\nabla H(x)\right\| > \varepsilon$ **Do**

            Determine step α along direction $-\nabla H(x)$

            $x \leftarrow x - \alpha \cdot \nabla H(x)$

      End While

      Return x

$End\ Function$

Box 3.1. *Basic gradient algorithm*

The mathematical field dealing with linear optimization problems is called Linear Programming (LP). Effective solving techniques – at least in practice – such as the simplex algorithm [DAN 90] or the interior point method [KAR 84] have been proposed for continuous linear problems. When certain variables are restricted by integer constraints (mixed or discrete problems), we have Integer Linear Programming (ILP). In general, these constraints make the problem more complex to solve and require the use of specific techniques such as Branch-and-Bound or Branch-and-Cut methods.

The range of applications of metaheuristics comes into play when traditional techniques (gradient, linear programming, etc.) fail to solve a problem. These methods, which started being used in the 80s, are built on some general concepts that enable them to adapt to a wide spectrum of problems. A metaheuristic procedure can be defined in many ways. Out of these, we will retain the one that describes it as an "iterative generation process which guides a subordinate heuristic by combining different concepts intelligently for exploring and exploiting the search space, learning strategies are used to structure information in order to find efficiently near-optimal solutions" [OSM 96].

Figure 3.1 illustrates optimization problems in relation to the characteristics of variables and constraints, and shows the range of applications of each solving technique.

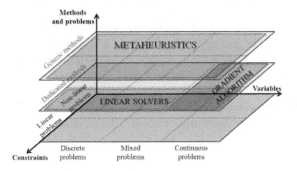

Figure 3.1. *Different optimization problems and their solving techniques*

3.2. Metaheuristics: basic notions

Metaheuristics are usually introduced by making a distinction between two broad categories of techniques: individual-based methods and population-based methods.

Individual-based techniques, sometimes called trajectory methods, aim to move within the search space by relying on a neighborhood system N which enables us to build a set of neighbor solutions $y \in N(x)$ starting from a current solution x.

Population-based techniques try to pool the pieces of information possessed by the people that make up the population in order to direct the search according to mechanisms that are specific to each metaheuristic.

Before describing some metaheuristic procedures in more detail, we will first define some general concepts which will subsequently help us understand how canwe design efficient techniques.

3.2.1. *Intensification and diversification*

The definition of metaheuristics proposed by Osman mentions the exploration and the exploitation of the search space. These two notions correspond to two strategies used to move within the search space, which are simultaneously clashing and complementary. The terms "intensification" (synonym of "exploitation") and "diversification" (synonym of "exploration") are frequently used in the metaheuristics microcosm.

Intensification consists of exploiting the knowledge that has been acquired since the beginning of the search. It is somehow as if some markers had been placed here and there in certain areas of the search space in order to focus most of the search on the sections considered most promising.

Diversification aims to seek new promising search areas. This consists of exploring, most often randomly, regions of the search area that are still completely unknown.

The blend, often subtle, of intensification and diversification simultaneously requires good knowledge of the problem at hand and a quite experienced metaheuristic designer. The positive outcome of the search relies heavily on these factors. This blend is produced by choosing the components of the metaheuristics and regulating the different parameters. [BLU 03] advances a general and clear description of the notions of exploration and exploitation, useful for those who want to know more about them.

3.2.2. *Neighborhood systems*

A neighborhood system is explicitly defined by a function $N : S \rightarrow 2^S$ that matches each solution $s \in S$ with a subset $N(s) \subset S$. In relation to each neighborhood system, we can define the set of local optima $S_N = S_N^- \cup S_N^+$ by means of $S_N^- = \{x \in S, \forall y \in N(x), H(x) \leq H(y)\}$ (local minima) and $S_N^+ = \{x \in S, \forall y \in N(x), H(x) \geq H(y)\}$ (local maxima).

This definition is weakened by two major flaws that render any neighborhood system simultaneously inapplicable and practically ineffective. Inapplicable because of the number of elements of S, it checks the enumeration of the solutions and thus prevents us *a fortiori* from being able to memorize the neighbors of each solution. It is ineffective because the definition does not incorporate any notion of proximity between two neighbor solutions. It actually proves to be crucial that two neighbor solutions are structurally as close as possible (i.e. that they share a lot of features) and that this fact corresponds, in economic terms, to two equally similar costs[1].

For these reasons neighborhood systems are in practice defined implicitly by relying, for example, on a mechanism aiming to modify the current solution as slightly as possible. We will use the term "basic move" to define some of these mechanisms. A basic move may consist, for example, of altering only one characteristic of the solution while leaving all the others unaltered.

Choosing a neighborhood system constitutes an important component of a metaheuristic procedure and its designer must pay very close attention to it. We will have the opportunity to describe simple and relatively generic basic move as well as more complex mechanisms, which enable us to define neighborhood system that are effective but more specific to a particular problem.

3.3. Individual-based metaheuristics

We decided to focus on the presentation of five individual-based optimization methods: local search, simulated annealing, the kangaroo algorithm, iterated local search and Tabu search. Naturally there are other and possibly more famous methods such as Variable Neighborhood Search (VNS) [MLA 97] or Greedy Randomized Adaptive Search Procedure (GRASP) [FEO 89], but we will let the reader discover them on his own.

3.3.1. *Local search*

Should we regard Local Search (LS) as a metaheuristic procedure? We may be tempted to claim so from a purely etymological point of view. LS is, actually, a general principle (Box 3.2) that can be applied to a substantially wide range of optimization problems. LS relies thus on a simple and general

---

1 The reader can find this claim justified in the "No Free Lunch" theorem [WOL 97].

concept, which however allows us only to exploit – and not to explore – the search space. In this sense, and according to the definition given by Osman, LS is not a metaheuristic. Nonetheless, this method is essential on many accounts:

– it is an ideal starting point to introduce metaheuristics (it is enough to add an exploratory mechanism to the principle of local search);

– LS is a major component of the hybridization of methods, a quite important technique we will come back to in more detail in Chapter 10.

We will describe two variants of LS: deterministic descent and stochastic descent.

3.3.1.1. *Deterministic descent*

Deterministic descent relies on a neighborhood system N. It consists of choosing – starting from an initial solution x_0 – one of the neighbor solutions, provided that it is strictly better. Thus, the chosen neighbor becomes the new reference solution. This process is repeated as long as the current solution can be improved. The basic algorithm of deterministic descent is shown in Box 3.2 within the context of a minimization problem.

Function LS (x_0) (deterministic version)

      Initialize $x \leftarrow x_0$

      While $x \notin S_N^-$ **Do**

            Choose $y \in N(x), H(y) < H(x)$

            $x \leftarrow y$

      End While

      Return x

End Function

Box 3.2. *Basic algorithm of local search*

A neighbor is most often chosen according to three approaches:

– choosing the best out of all the improving-neighbors (Best Improvement (BI));

– choosing the first improving-neighbor we come across (First Improvement (FI));

– randomly choosing one out of all the improving-neighbors (Random Improvement (RI)).

Employing one of these approaches implies the ability to enumerate the neighborhood of a solution: fully for policies BI and RI, and partially for policy FI.

The BI or FI approaches are deterministic in that, starting from the same initial solution, LS always creates the same local minimum. On the contrary, the RI approach is used to generate local minima that will be different from each other *a priori*. In the latter case, applying several LSs one after the other and memorizing the best local minimum obtained from each of them will smoothly lead us into the field of metaheuristics.

3.3.1.2. *Stochastic descent*

Stochastic descent is an alternative method that allows us to avoid enumerating the neighbors. This procedure consists, for each repetition, of randomly and uniformly choosing a solution y in the neighborhood of the current solution x and in accepting it as the new current solution only if it is better. The basic algorithm is shown in Box 3.3. It employs two extra variables: $nb\_failure$ and $itermax$. The former counts the number of consecutive failures in the search for an improving-neighbor whereas the latter sets the threshold number of consecutive failures after which the algorithm is terminated.

Let us deal with the most unfavorable case, in which only one improving-neighbor y can be found in the neighborhood of x. Let us define X as the random variable that counts the number of draws with replacement necessary to draw y for the first time. Then the inequality $P(X \leq itermax) \geq p_0$, where $itermax$ is the unknown, represents the least number of times we have to draw a neighbor if we want to find the improving-neighbor y with a given probability P_0. Solving it gives us $itermax \approx -\ln(1-p_0) \times |N(x)|$. So Gerard Fleury [FLE 93], the designer of the kangaroo algorithm[2], suggests choosing $itermax = 0.7 \times |N(x)|$, which corresponds to a probability of around

$$p_0 = \frac{1}{2}.$$

---

2 The kangaroo algorithm, which is an iterated stochastic descent, is described in detail in section 3.3.3.

This formula is quite interesting in that it provides its user with an intuitive and probability-based means of setting the exploitation rate that we want to incorporate into a local search.

Function $LS(x_0)$ (stochastic version)

                Initialize $x \leftarrow x_0$

       Set *nb _ failure* $\leftarrow 0$

       While *nb _ failure* $<$ *itermax* **Do**

                Randomly and uniformly choose $y \in N(x)$

              If $H(y) < H(x)$ Then

                    $x \leftarrow y$

                    nb _ failure $\leftarrow 0$

            Else

                    nb _ failure $\leftarrow$ *nb _ failure* $+ 1$

            End If

       End While

Return x

End Function

Box 3.3. *Basic algorithm of stochastic descent*

These two kinds of descents have each advantages and drawbacks. Deterministic descent relies on listing, at least partially, the neighborhood whereas stochastic descent can never guarantee that we will obtain a local minimum. In the next section, we will describe one of the emblematic metaheuristics, namely simulated annealing, which may be seen as an extension of stochastic descent that incorporates an exploration mechanism.

3.3.2. Simulated Annealing

Simulated Annealing (SA) appeared at the beginning of the 1980s simultaneously in two papers, [KIR 83] and [CER 85]. It is inspired by a metallurgical process that consists of a material going through a cycle of slow cooling down and heating (annealing), resulting in the minimization of its energy.

In relation to stochastic descent, simulated annealing introduces a new parameter, i.e. temperature T. The general idea of simulated annealing consists of being able to accept non-improving neighbors as well, according to a probability $p(\Delta H,T)$ that depends on the cost degradation $\Delta H = H(y) - H(x)$ and the current temperature T. The most typical criterion used is the Metropolis dynamic ($p(\Delta H,T) = e^{-\frac{\Delta H}{T}}$). Throughout the algorithm the temperature decreases towards 0, causing the probability of accepting unfavorable transition to decrease progressively towards 0.

The basic algorithm of simulated annealing is shown in Box 3.4. Function $RND( )$ is used to generate a real number within the interval [0; 1]. We can identify here one of the features specific to metaheuristics: the stopping criterion. In the context of annealing, the most used criteria are the maximum number of iterations, the maximum number of non-improving iterations, the acquisition of a solution deemed qualitatively satisfactory, reaching a pre-established final temperature, etc.

Function SA(x_0)
        Initialize $x \leftarrow x_0$
        $Rx \leftarrow x$
        Initialize T
        While *the stopping criterion is not satisfied* **Do**
                Randomly and uniformly choose $y \in N(x)$
                If $H(y) < H(x)$ Then
                      $x \leftarrow y$
                      If $H(y) < H(Rx)$ Then
                            $Rx \leftarrow y$
                      End If
                Else
                      If $RND( ) < p(\Delta H,T)$ Then
                            $x \leftarrow y$
                      End If
                End If
                Update T
        End While
        Return Rx
End Function

Box 3.4. *Basic algorithm of simulated annealing*

SA has specific characteristics. It has the ability to "forget" the initial solution. Thus, it is not necessary to envisage an efficient heuristic in order to generate it. Theoretically, there is no need to deal with a record state (if the temperature decreases slowly enough, the record solution is deemed to be the one obtained at the end of the algorithm), but we strongly advise to do it in practice.

There are several ways of updating the temperature. In general we can find two categories of SA: the homogeneous one, where temperature decreases in stages (we try to reach equilibrium at every temperature level before cooling down again) and the inhomogeneous one, where temperature decreases for each iteration (according to a geometric law for example).

SA is criticized mainly because it needs to handle temperature well in order to be effective. On the other hand, once correctly calibrated, it turns out to be very efficient. Its strength lies in that the search in the domain of solutions relies on intense exploration at the beginning of the algorithm (high temperature) that progressively wears off and is completely replaced by exploitation by the end of the algorithm.

In conclusion, let us note that SA is, from a theoretical point of view, an algorithm. [HAJ 88] showed the convergence to the set of global optima, in terms of probability, on condition that the temperature decreases slowly enough. This process of decreasing, being in most cases impossible to satisfy, is practically used as a heuristic. Lastly, if the temperature is constant and null, no unfavorable transition is accepted and simulated annealing performs as a stochastic descent.

The following metaheuristic is defined, on a historical level, as a sequence of stochastic descents and belongs to the family of stochastic algorithms of the same kind as simulated annealing. It is the kangaroo algorithm.

3.3.3. *The kangaroo algorithm*

Historically, the kangaroo algorithm was introduced by Gérard Fleury [FLE 93] as a succession of stochastic descents linked by a mechanism quite cleverly called "jump". A jump simply consists of perturbing the solution obtained at the conclusion of a descent and in using the new solution thus built as the initial solution of the following descent. The idea around which this method pivots is to perform each descent in the neighborhood of the preceding one. In that regard the jump must be big enough to allow us to get out of the valley where the descent is trapped (factor of exploration for the search space) and small enough to not completely forget the last trajectory in the search space (factor of exploitation in the space of local minima). The kangaroo algorithm uses two neighborhoods: one for the descent (N) and the other for the jump (N'). The basic kangaroo algorithm is shown in Box 3.5.

Function KA(x_0, itermax)

        Initialize $x \leftarrow x_0$

        $Rx \leftarrow x$

        While *the stopping criterion is not satisfied* **Do**

                $x \leftarrow [Stochastic] LS(x, itermax)$ // descent phase

            If $H(x) < H(Rx)$ Then

                  $Rx \leftarrow x$

            End If

            Randomly and uniformly choose $y \in N'(x)$ // jump phase

            $x \leftarrow y$

        End While

        Return Rx

End Function

Box 3.5. *Basic kangaroo algorithm*

Very often, the neighborhood N' consists of applying the neighborhood N a certain number of times (for example 3 times, while accepting unfavorable transitions).

Like simulated annealing, the kangaroo procedure is regarded as an algorithm. It converges, in terms of probability, to an optimal solution under certain conditions in relation to the neighborhood N'. These conditions are quite easy to satisfy in practice, unlike those of simulated annealing (accessibility properties – we must be able to link each pair of solutions with a chain of neighbors – and reversibility properties – $x \in N'(y) \Rightarrow y \in N'(x)$).

However, a wise programmer will define a stopping criterion while taking into account a maximum calculation time. In practice, the kangaroo algorithm will stop quite often before finding the Holy Grail! Anyway, even if we reach the optimum, we will probably not realize it since this kind of algorithm is not characterized by any process that proves optimality. In addition to these purely theoretical considerations, the kangaroo algorithm has two more advantages over simulated annealing that will thrill the occasional user. On the one hand, it is much easier to set. The stage is the main parameter of the kangaroo algorithm and it is easy enough to determine a value that works well (see section 3.3.1.2). Moreover, it allows us to obtain solutions of good quality from the beginning of the algorithm. The informed user will, however, prefer the SA procedure, which is generally more effective as soon as its concepts are mastered.

Methodologically, the kangaroo algorithm belongs to the category of iterated local searches. We will explain in the following section why the performance of the kangaroo algorithm can be significantly improved by modifying the instruction $y \in N'(x)$ into $y \in N'(Rx)$ and we will see how it is possible to do even better!

3.3.4. Iterated local search

[LOU 03] had the great merit of grouping the procedures of sequential local searches, which have been used for several years in different forms. The designers proposed a basic algorithm both simple and clear but also generic enough to group under its umbrella several trajectory methods. This algorithm is called iterated local search (ILS). ILS aims to execute a "step" in the restricted space of the local minima (S_N^-). By studying the basic algorithm (Box 3.6), we realize that an iteration can be broken down into three phases:

Function ILS(x_0)

    $x \leftarrow x_0$

    $x^* \leftarrow LS(x)$

    Repeat

        $x' \leftarrow perturbation(x^*, history)$

        $x'' \leftarrow LS(x')$

        $x^* \leftarrow AcceptanceCriterion(x^*, x'', history)$

    Until one of the stopping conditions is satisfied

    Return x^*

End Function

Box 3.6. *Basic algorithm of ILS*

– the perturbation phase is the mechanism enabling ILS to escape the local minima by perturbing the current local minimum x^*. We then obtain a new solution x', which has no reason to be a local minimum;

– the optimization phase consists of applying a local search (which may be deterministic or stochastic) starting from x'. We then obtain a new local minimum $x^{*'}$;

– the last phase is a phase of choice, thanks to which we can determine which of the two local minima will be kept for the following iteration. The Random Walk criterion (RW) consists of choosing the most recent of two local minima ($x^* \leftarrow x^{*'}$) and allows us to explore the space S_N^-. On the contrary, the criterion called "Better" consists of systematically keeping the better one amongst two. Between the two extremes represented by these two strategies, there is a range of intermediate solutions, such as the application of a simulated-annealing-style process that can be employed.

Let us reconsider for a moment the kangaroo algorithm, which is completely integrated into the ILS process with an LS component, which is a stochastic descent, and an acceptance criterion of the RW kind. [DER 02] suggested replacing the instruction of the kangaroo algorithm randomly and uniformly choosing $y \in N'(x)$ with $y \in N'(Rx)$. This minor alteration allows us to improve significantly the performance of the metaheuristic (despite the fact that the theoretical convergence is lost). In the ILS paradigm this amounts to defining an acceptance criterion of the "Better" kind.

The results obtained in the literature, whether for ILS or for the kangaroo algorithm, are in perfect agreement. The Better criterion generally turns out to be a much more effective choice than the RW one. A criterion of the simulated annealing kind is naturally a little harder to master but it will most often outclass the Better criterion as soon as a large enough number of searches are performed.

3.3.5. *Tabu Search*

Tabu Search (TS) [GLO 86] is a metaheuristic procedure that essentially relies, as does simulated annealing, on local search. It consists of sampling the domain of the solutions by employing an extremely simple principle. At each iteration, a new solution in the neighborhood of the current one is chosen according to the criterion formulated below. Among all the non-tabu neighbor solutions, we select the one that minimizes the cost function. TS differs from local search in two fundamental ways:

– a neighbor solution can be chosen even if its cost is superior to that of the current one. It is this mechanism that allows us to extract local minima;

– the tabu list is a recollection of the last solutions encountered during exploration. Its role is to prevent the method from cycling around some solutions. In practice, the size of this list is generally fixed and managed according to the FIFO rule.

The basic algorithm of TS is shown in Box 3.7.

$Function\ Tabu\ Search\ (x_0)$

$\quad\quad\quad x \leftarrow x_0$

$\quad\quad\quad Rx \leftarrow x$

$\quad\quad\quad TabuList \leftarrow \varnothing$

$\quad\quad\quad$**While** *the stopping condition is not satisfied* **Do**

$\quad\quad\quad\quad\quad\quad$Choose $x' \in V(x)\,/\,H(x') = \min\big(H(y), y \in V(x) \setminus TabuList\big)$

$\quad\quad\quad\quad\quad\quad x \leftarrow x'$

$\quad\quad\quad\quad\quad\quad TabuList \leftarrow TabuList \cup \{x\}$

$\quad\quad\quad\quad\quad\quad$**If** $H(x') < H(Rx)$ **Then**

$\quad\quad\quad\quad\quad\quad\quad\quad\quad Rx \leftarrow x'$

$\quad\quad\quad\quad\quad\quad$**End If**

$\quad\quad\quad$**End While**

$\quad\quad\quad$Return Rx

$End\ Function$

Box 3.7. *Basic algorithm of TS*

3.4. Population-based metaheuristics

The objective of population-based methods is to initiate an interaction between the individuals that make up a population in order to generate new solutions. We focus on three methods that quite fittingly represent the principles that can be used: evolutionary algorithms, the ant colony algorithm and particle swarm optimization.

3.4.1. *Evolutionary algorithms*

This term groups a whole family of metaheuristics whose most famous members are genetic algorithms [HOL 75, GOL 89] and differential evolution algorithms [STO 97]. These metaheuristic procedures rely on Darwin's theory of evolution. They attempt to make a population evolve, generation by generation, so that its individuals optimize a cost function which represents their degree of adaptation to the natural environment. The basic algorithm is shown in Box 3.8.

Evolutionary algorithms are characterized by various phases. Though there are a large number of variants but here we will only introduce some general principles in order to better come to grips with the principle of these methods:

Function Evolutionary_ Algorithm()

    Initialization: creation of the initial population G_0

    Assess the adaptation degree of each individual

    $Rx \leftarrow x / H(x) = \min(H(y), y \in G_0)$

    For *k from 1 to MaxGeneration* **Do**

    Parents' selection in G_{k-1}

            Reproduction Phase (fathering of children agents of

                    crossover and mutation)

            Assess the adaptation degree of each child

            If necessary, update the record state Rx

            Replacement phase: creation of the generation G_k

    End For

    Return Rx

End Function

Box 3.8. *General principle of evolutionary algorithms*

– the initialization phase consists of generating the initial population. The first individuals are often created randomly so that it may have great genetic diversity;

– the selection phase consists of choosing the parents that will reproduce, while improving the chances of the best of them. The Roulette and the Tournament principles are often employed. A parent is allocated one of the Roulette sections, which may be more or less important, and is chosen when the ball stops on his or her section. The tournament consists of having parents face each other in a duel (the best parent having a greater chance of winning) so that only two finalists remain;

– the reproduction phase consists of the fathering of children from the chromosome of the chosen parents. It includes the key operators, i.e. crossover and mutation. Crossover is a generally binary operator that tries to preserve the characteristics shared by two parents in order to generate one or two children who will hopefully be better. This operator is, thus, an exploitation factor. According to an established mutation rate, each infant's chromosome may undergo a genetic mutation. This unary operator consists, in general, of modifying the information carried on a locus randomly. Mutation is an exploration factor;

– the replacement phase simply consists of creating the generation by choosing out of the parents and children that are part of it, those who will survive. The number of individuals that make up each generation may be constant. It is advisable to preserve the best individuals to ensure a better convergence of the algorithm (elitist strategy). It is equally desirable to randomly keep some individuals in order to maintain genetic diversity.

3.4.2. *The ant colony algorithm*

The ant colony algorithms [COL 91] draw their inspiration from the cooperative behavior of ants. These have developed very complex mechanisms in order to find the shortest way from their anthill to a food source. Ants release on their path a trail of pheromones that attract their fellow creatures passing nearby. The pheromone trails weaken over time and we can see that if there are several paths between the anthill and the food source, the shortest trail will tend to reinforce itself and to become more and more appealing to the detriment of the other paths where the pheromones will progressively get weaker and weaker, and finally disappear. The principle of the ant colony algorithm is displayed in Box 3.9. [DOR 97] shows how ant colonies can be used to solve the traveling salesman problem.

The basic ant colony algorithm is based on two rules that regulate pheromone updating:

– *Local updating*: Each ant progressively builds up a solution, element by element, taking a series of decisions in a graph. Each decision is taken in relation to a probability that takes into account the relevance of the choice (local optimization) and the pheromone rate associated to it. The ant, in turn, releases its own pheromones to mark its choice.

– *Global updating*: Once all the ants have labored, the solutions they have built are evaluated. The pheromone trail corresponding to the best solution that has been found since the beginning of the algorithm is then reinforced.

Function Ant _ Colony()

        Initialization

        While *the stopping condition is not satisfied* **Do**

            Place the ants at the beginning of the graph

            While *the ants have not terminated their solution* **Do**

                Each ant applies a decision rule to

                choose the next element and releases its pheromones

                according to the local pheromone updating rule

        End While

            Evaluate the solutions created by the ants

            If necessary, update the record state *Rx*

            Apply the rule of global pheromone updating

        End While

        Return *Rx*

End Function

Box 3.9. *General principle of the ant colony algorithm*

3.4.3. *Particle Swarm Optimization*

Particle Swarm Optimization (PSO) is a metaheuristic advanced by [EBE 95]. While it was initially conceived as a solving technique for continuous optimization problems, several approaches such as [CLE 04], have been described in order to adapt this metaheuristic to combinatorial optimization problems. PSO is a population-based method in which its individuals, here dubbed particles, try to imitate the behavior of bird flocks or fish schools.

The mechanism of this metaheuristic can be described in a local space comparable to $\mathbb{R}^n$. Each particle i has at every instant t a position $x_i(t)$ and a velocity $v_i(t)$. It has also the ability to remember its best previous position p_i. Lastly, particles can communicate with a group of "friend" particles and thus find out the optimal position g_i, located within this group. In this context, the movement of a particle is the compromise of three tendencies:

– an individualistic tendency: The particle moves around at its own velocity according to a coefficient c_1;

– a conservative tendency: The particle tries to return to its best position according to a coefficient c_2;

– a "panurgian" tendency: The particle tries to follow its best "friend" particle according to a coefficient c_3.

In the interval between t and $t + 1$, particles move around according to the rules stated below, for each component $d \in [\![1, n]\!]$:

$$v_{i,d}(t+1) = c_1 v_{i,d}(t) + c_2 RND()\left[p_{i,d} - x_{i,d}(t)\right] + c_3 RND()\left[g_{i,d} - x_{i,d}(t)\right] \quad [3.1]$$

$$x_{i,d}(t+1) = x_{i,d}(t) + v_{i,d}(t+1) \quad [3.2]$$

The basic algorithm of PSO is shown in Box 3.10.

Function PSO()

    For each particle i

        Determine its starting position $x_i(0)$ and its velocity $v_i(0)$

        $p_i \leftarrow x_i(0)$

    End For

    While *the stopping condition is not satisfied* **Do**

        For each particle i

            Determine the position of the friend particles g_i

            Move the particle by applying [3.1] and [3.2]

            If necessary, update p_i

        End For

    End While

    Return $p_{i*} / H(p_{i*}) = \min_i H(p_i)$

EndFunction

Box 3.10. *General principle of PSO*

In addition to the choice of the coefficients c_1, c_2 and c_3, another paramount factor is the selection of friend particles. According to the original version, each particle is deemed a friend particle. This version, called "global model", has been quickly outclassed by local methods since, in the former, the swarm tends to converge too rapidly to a local minimum and ends up trapped in it.

3.5. Conclusion

Metaheuristics provides us with a general solving framework. The significant strength of its methods depends on their wide range of applications. The following chapter aims to show definitively how these techniques can be developed by presenting a simple case. The problem we chose to examine is not a problem in itself but a category of them, called permutation problems. They are all problems that feature a certain order as their solution, such as the order in which cities are visited by the traveling salesman or the order in which parts enter the workshop in the permutation flow-shop problem.

4

A First Implementation
of Metaheuristics

After giving an outline of metaheuristics, we intend to show more definitively how these procedures can quite easily be set up. This first implementation allows us, with relatively little effort, to obtain results that are already comparatively satisfactory for many of the logistic problems we have introduced. The only condition that needs to be satisfied is that we should be able to represent the solution as a list of objects. This inventory of objects may characterize a solution to our problem (list of cities to be visited, list of products to be manufactured, etc.), in which case we will talk about "direct solution representation". It may also represent an order that allows us to create a solution to our problem (the first stage of a construction heuristic, for example – we will find more of them in the following chapters). The representation of the solution will then be called indirect. After describing how a list of objects can be represented, we will define the components necessary for the conception of a first metaheuristic, namely the initialization phase (generation of one or many initial solution(s)) and the optimization phase (techniques employed to build new solutions from existing ones). Some metaheuristics will then be described in more detail.

4.1. Representing a list of objects

Let us consider an optimization problem in which a solution corresponds to the creation of a set of objects $\{o_1, o_2, ..., o_n\}$ in a specific order. Therefore, there are as many solutions as there may be orders. Mathematically, a solution is modeled through a permutation of the interval

$[\![1,n]\!]$ within itself, n indicating the number of objects we are dealing with. For example, the permutation $\sigma = [3,6,8,2,1,4,7,5]$ corresponds to the creation of the object o_3, then of the object o_6, and so forth. On the other hand, in terms of informatics, there are several ways of storing this permutation, as shown in Figure 4.1:

– we can declare an array *ord* in which *ord*$[i]$ will designate the ith object in the permutation σ. Thus, $ord[1] = o_3$, $ord[2] = o_6$, etc.;

– we can declare an array *pos* in which *pos*$[i]$ indicates the position in which the object o_i is located in the permutation σ. Thus, $pos[1] = 5$, $pos[2] = 4$, etc.;

– we can declare two arrays *prec* and *succ* which indicate, respectively, the object preceding and the object following the object o_i in the permutation σ. So, $prec[3] = \varnothing$, $prec[6] = o_3$, $succ[3] = o_6$, $succ[6] = o_8$, etc. Clearly, the first and the last objects are not preceded or followed by any object. We will decide then to store the value 0. Let us point out that in the specific case of the TSP the solution is cyclic. Thus, each object is both preceded and followed ($prec[3] = o_5$).

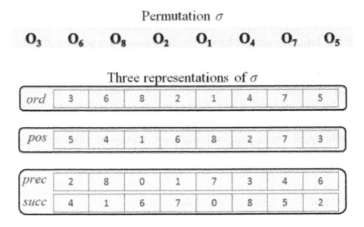

Figure 4.1. *Illustration of a permutation and of some representations*

The choice of the most suitable representation will essentially depend on the incorporation of advanced components into the metaheuristics.

Sometimes it may even turn out to be useful to manipulate several of these representations simultaneously. In the context of this chapter, any representation will serve our purpose. From now on we will use the *order* representation, which seems the most intuitive to us. We will leave it to the reader, as a sort of exercise, to make the necessary changes to the other kinds of representations.

4.2. The implementation of a local search

Local search is an iterative improving method. Like most methods of this kind, it inevitably involves an initial solution from which we can build a neighbor which we may either accept or refuse depending on whether it improves or not the current solution. In this section, we intend to devise a stochastic descent that we will be able to apply whenever the representation of a solution is of the permutation kind.

4.2.1. *The construction of an initial solution*

When we work on a specific logistic problem, we can make use of its properties to generate rapidly good solutions through construction heuristics. While waiting to gain access to this kind of knowledge, we can hardly do anything but resort to the random generation of solutions. In the case of a permutation, that can be done with the Fisher–Yates shuffle (Box 4.1), which has the advantage of generating a random unbiased permutation starting from any permutation in linear time. The generation of an initial solution is shown in Box 4.2.

```
// permutation of two elements in pos1 and pos2 in the array X
Procedure Exchange (X : array, pos1 : integer, pos2 : integer)
        Dim tmp : integer
        tmp ← X[pos1]
        X[pos1] ← X[pos2]
        X[pos2] ← tmp
End Procedure

Procedure Fisher_Yates (X : array(1..n), n : integer)
        Dim i, j : integer
        Dim tmp : integer
```

> **For** i **from** n **to 2 through** -1 **Do**
> $$j \leftarrow alea(1,i)$$
> Call *Exchange* (X,i,j)
> **End For**
> **End Procedure**

Box 4.1. *The Fisher–Yates algorithm*

> **Procedure** *Generate initial solution*
> Dim i : integer
> **For** i **from** 1 **to** n **Do**
> $$X[i] \leftarrow i$$
> **End For**
> Call *Fisher_Yates* (X,n)
> **End Procedure**

Box 4.2. *Generation of a random initial solution*

4.2.2. Description of basic moves

Local search is based on the notion of neighborhood, which enables it to generate new solutions, called neighbor solutions, from the current one. We introduce here the neighborhood systems most often employed for permutations: the moves of exchange, insertion and inversion. These are displayed in Figure 4.2, where we consider the permutation $\sigma = [3,6,8,2,1,4,7,5]$ as the current solution:

– the exchange move consists of exchanging the two objects of σ located in positions p_1 and p_2 ($p_1 < p_2$). For example, exchanging the objects in positions 3 and 6 yields the permutation $\sigma' = [3,6,4,2,1,8,7,5]$;

– the insertion move consists of removing the element of σ in position p_1 and in reinserting it into position p_2 ($p_1 \neq p_2$). In relation to our example, object 8 is inserted between objects 4 and 7, which allows us to build the permutation $\sigma' = [3,6,2,1,4,8,7,5]$;

– the inversion move consists of inverting the order of the objects of σ located between positions p_1 et p_2 ($p_1 < p_2$). In relation to our example, the order of objects 8,2,1,4 is inverted. We thus obtain the permutation $\sigma' = [3,6,4,1,2,8,7,5]$. This kind of move is better known in the literature on the TSP as the 2–opt move. We will have the opportunity to come back to this point when we tackle that part.

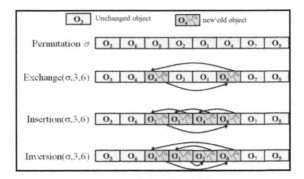

Figure 4.2. *Illustration of the exchange, insertion, and inversion moves*

The exchange move can be performed by means of the procedure *Exchange* (σ, i, j), which we described above (see Box 4.1). The insertion and inversion moves are displayed in detail in Boxes 4.3 and 4.4.

```
// insertion of the object in position pos1 into position pos2 in the array X
Procedure insertion (X : array, pos1 : integer, pos2 : integer)
        Dim i : integer
        Dim tmp : integer
        tmp ← X[pos1]
        If pos1 < pos2 Then        // left shift
                For i from pos1 to pos2−1 Do
                        X[i] ← X[i+1]
                End For
        Else                       // right shift
                For i from pos1 to pos2+1 par −1 Do
                        X[i] ← X[i−1]
                End For
        End If
        X[pos2] ← tmp
End Procedure
```

Box 4.3. *Insertion moves*

```
// inversion of objects in positions pos1 and pos2 in the array X
Procedure inversion (X : array, pos1 : integer, pos2 : integer)
        Dim i, j : integer
        i ← pos1
        j ← pos2
          While i < j Do
                  Call Exchange (X, i, j)
                  i ← i + 1
                  j ← j − 1
        End While
End Procedure
```

Box 4.4. *Inversion moves*

4.2.3. *The implementation of stochastic descent (LS)*

The basic algorithm of stochastic descent (see Box 3.3) mentions the use of two solutions x and y, the former representing the current solution and the latter the neighbor solution. This presupposes the declaration of two arrays to store the two permutations, with array copying when the neighbor solution is optimal ($x \leftarrow y$). Actually, we will declare only one array which will contain in turns the current permutation as well as its neighbor. Because of this we exploit the fact that, in case we wish to go backwards, it is easy to undo each of the three moves on condition that we remember which one was performed. So, $Exchange(X, pos1, pos2)$ can undo $Exchange(X, pos1, pos2)$, $Insertion(X, pos2, pos1)$ can undo $Insertion(X, pos1, pos2)$, and $Inversion(X, pos1, pos2)$ can undo $Inversion(X, pos1, pos2)$. We define as $Apply\_V(X, pos1, pos2)$ the call to one of the three neighborhoods which allows us to move, in X, from the current solution to the neighbor one. We define as $Undo\_V(X, pos1, pos2)$ the opposite procedure, which lets us go back to the current solution in X (pay attention to the position of the parameters for the insertion move!).

Stochastic descent also brings into play the parameter *itermax*, which represents the maximum number of consecutive failures in the search for a qualitatively better neighbor. We have suggested setting down

Itermax $\approx 0.7 \times |N(x)|$ where $N(x)$ designates the set of neighbors of x. In the case of the *Exchange* $(X, pos1, pos2)$ and *Inversion* $(X, pos1, pos2)$ moves, the parameters $pos1$ and $pos2$ have a symmetric role. Thus, we can hypothesize that $pos1$ is the smaller of the two ($pos1 < pos2$). Starting from a permutation of x it is then possible to create $\dfrac{n(n-1)}{2}$ different neighbor permutations, among which we will consider $|N(x)| \approx \dfrac{1}{2}n^2$. The symmetric role of the parameters is no longer valid for the insertion move. In this case, we only suppose that $pos1 \neq pos2$ and we consider $|N(x)| = n(n-1) \approx n^2$.

Procedure $LS(X : array, n : integer)$
    dim $nb\_failure$: integer   // failure counter
    dim *itermax* : integer   // maximum number of failures allowed
    dim $pos1$, $pos2$: integer   // positions to be modified
    dim Hx , Hy : integer   // cost of current and neighbor solutions
    Call *Generate Initial Solution* (X,n)
    $Hx \leftarrow Calcul\_cost(X,n)$
    $itermax \leftarrow \lfloor 0.7n^2 \rfloor$ (exchange, inversion) or $\lfloor 0.35n^2 \rfloor$ (insertion) or
    $nb\_failure \leftarrow 0$
    While $nb\_failure < itermax$ **Do**
        $pos1 \leftarrow alea(1,n)$, $pos2 \leftarrow alea(1,n)$
        While $pos1 = pos2$ **Do**
            $pos2 \leftarrow alea(1,n)$
        End While
        $Apply\_V (X, pos1, pos2)$
        $Hy \leftarrow Calcul\_cost(X,n)$
        If $H(y) < H(x)$ **Then**   // success: neighbor solution is kept
            $Hx \leftarrow Hy$
            $nb\_failure \leftarrow 0$
        Else   // failure: return to current solution
            $Undo\_V (X, pos1, pos2)$
            $nb\_failure \leftarrow nb\_failure + 1$
        End If
    End While
End Procedure

Box 4.5. *Stochastic descent applied to permutations*

In Box 4.5 we examine in some detail the case of local search being applied to permutations. Function $Calcul\_cost(X,n)$, which estimates the cost of permutation X, is the only component of the algorithm that depends on the problem considered.

4.3. The implementation of individual-based metaheuristics

We are going to describe the setting up of simulated annealing and of an iterated local search.

4.3.1. Simulated annealing (SA)

SA is a stochastic descent in which we handle an extra parameter, namely the temperature T, and we can accept some unfavorable transitions in relation to a probability depending on the temperature. Consequently, it is relatively easy to transform a stochastic descent into SA. It is enough to handle temperature instead of the failure counter and to add the possibility of accepting an unfavorable transition. It is equally advisable to manage a record state, which is initialized by the initial solution and eventually updated, should a transition be favorable.

One of the simplest rules for managing temperature is to employ a geometric law. Throughout the algorithm, the temperature T goes from an initial state $T_{beginning}$ to a final state T_{end}. At each iteration, the temperature is updated by being multiplied by a coefficient slightly smaller than 1 $\left(T^{(k+1)} \leftarrow \mu \times T^{(k)}\right)$.

The initial temperature can be measured by means of the following proposition: we set a 50% chance of accepting a solution that degrades the objective function by 1 unit ($\Delta H = H(y) - H(x) = 1$). In other words, we solve the equation $\exp\left(\dfrac{-\Delta H}{T}\right) = \dfrac{1}{2}$, which yields $T_{beginning} = \dfrac{1}{\ln 2} \approx 1.44$. As for the final temperature, we similarly set one chance out of n^2, yielding $T_{end} = \dfrac{1}{2 \ln n}$. Lastly, we want the annealing to stop after the execution of a set number of *itermax* iterations. We obtain then $T^{(iter\,max)} = T_{end}$, or

$\mu^{itermax} T_{beginning} = T_{end}$, from which we obtain $\mu = {}^{itermax}\sqrt{\dfrac{T_{end}}{T_{beginning}}}$.

The detailed algorithm of SA is given in Box 4.6.

Procedure $SA(X : array, n : integer, itermax : integer)$

      dim T , T_{end} , μ : float   // parameters for temperature management

      dim $pos1$, $pos2$: integer   // positions to be modified

      dim Hx , Hy : integer   // cost of current and neighbor solutions

      dim RX : array, Hr : integer   // record solution and its cost

      Call *Generate Initial Solution* (X,n)

      $Hx \leftarrow Calcul\_cost(X,n)$

      $RX \leftarrow X$, $Hr \leftarrow Hx$

      $T \leftarrow \dfrac{1}{\ln(2)}$, $T_{fin} \leftarrow \dfrac{1}{2\ln(n)}$, $\mu \leftarrow {}^{itermax}\sqrt{\dfrac{T}{T_{fin}}}$

      While $T > T_{fin}$ **Do**

          $pos1 \leftarrow alea(1,n)$, $pos2 \leftarrow alea(1,n)$

          While $pos1 = pos2$ **Do**

              $pos2 \leftarrow alea(1,n)$

          End While

          $Apply\_V (X, pos1, pos2)$

          $Hy \leftarrow Calcul\_cost(X,n)$

          If $H(y) < H(x)$ **Then**   // success: neighbor solution is kept

              If $H(y) < H(RX)$ **Then**

                  $RX \leftarrow y$, $Hr \leftarrow Hy$

              End If

              $Hx \leftarrow Hy$

          Else   // failure: acceptance test

              If $\left(RND() < \exp\left(\dfrac{H(x) - H(y)}{T} \right) \right)$ **then**

                  $Hx \leftarrow Hy$

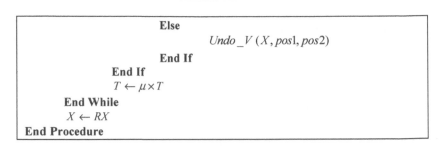

Box 4.6. *Detailed algorithm of simulated annealing*

4.3.2. *Iterated local search (ILS)*

In Box 4.7 we show a detailed algorithm of iterated local search in which the stopping test corresponds to a pre-established number of descents (parameter *nb _ desc*). ILS includes three components:

– Perturbation (x^*, history): We intend to apply three times one of the neighborhood systems we have defined.

– *LS* (x'): We will employ the stochastic descent procedure (Box 4.5). We simply have to remove the instruction that generates a random solution at the beginning of the descent. This call will be performed only once at the beginning of ILS.

– Acceptance Criterion (x^*, $x^{*\,'}$, *history*): We will choose to keep the better of two local minima ("Better" criterion). To implement the "Random Walk" criterion, it is enough to perform systematically the instructions $X \leftarrow Y$, $Hx \leftarrow Hy$. The difference between the two criteria stems exclusively from the last test.

4.14. Conclusion

In this chapter we have organized all the elements necessary to implement a metaheuristic all in all rudimentary but already able to provide results of good quality. As a rule of thumb, concerning the TSP or the flowshop problems, metaheuristics let us find quite easily solutions around 1% of the optimal one. To cross this threshold, we will have to start incorporating some components that are more sophisticated and specific to the problem.

We will provide some results in support of these remarks at the end of the two following chapters, which are rightly dedicated to a more in-depth study of these two problems.

In an industrial context, where data are uncertain or imprecise and a certain number of simplifying hypotheses are made, the results obtained will often be satisfactory enough to justify the decision taken.

Procedure $ILS(X : array, n : integer, nb\_desc : integer)$
      dim $pos1$, $pos2$: integer   // positions to be modified
      dim Y : array   // new local minimum
      dim Hx, Hy : integer   // cost of the current and neighbor solutions
      dim desc, i : integer   // loop variables

      Call *Generate Initial Solution* (X, n)
      Call $LS(X, n)$
      $Hx \leftarrow Calcul\_cost(X, n)$
      For *desc* **from** 1 **to** *nb_desc* **Do**
            // perturbation phase: 3 applications of one of the neighborhoods
            $Y \leftarrow X$
            For *i* **from** 1 **to** 3 **Do**
                  $pos1 \leftarrow alea(1, n)$, $pos2 \leftarrow alea(1, n)$
                  While $pos1 = pos2$ **Do**
                      $pos2 \leftarrow alea(1, n)$
                End While
                $Apply\_V$ $(Y, pos1, pos2)$
            End For
            // local search phase
            Call $LS(Y, n)$
            $Hy \leftarrow Calcul\_cost(Y, n)$
            // acceptance criterion phase: "Better" criterion
            If $Hy < Hx$ **Then**   // success: neighbor solution is kept
                  $X \leftarrow Y$, $Hx \leftarrow Hy$
            End If
      End For
End Procedure

Box 4.7. *Detailed algorithm of ILS*

PART 2

Advanced Notions

5

The Traveling Salesman Problem

The traveling salesman problem (TSP) is to combinatorial optimization problems what Formula One is to the motor industry: a formidable laboratory that pours its stream of ideas into the whole of the field. On one hand, this problem constitutes a showcase. By virtue of its simplicity, it is regularly employed to illustrate the mechanisms of an emerging metaheuristic or as a tutorial (particle swarm, ant colonies, etc.). On the other hand, the intensive studies dedicated to it have enabled us to devise techniques, simultaneously innovative and highly efficient. Certain mathematical properties of the TSP have been used to conceive metaheuristic components that become more and more effective. Several ideas, originally drawn from the TSP, have afterwards been applied to other problems. It is some of these ideas that we will focus on in this chapter.

5.1. Representing a solution: the two-level tree structure

It is handy to represent the solution of a TSP, which we will call a "tour", as a permutation of its set of n cities (for the sake of simplification, we will continue to use this representation for the rest of the chapter). However, many others have been used in the literature on the TSP. Out of these, we will introduce the two-level tree structure, which has turned out to be as useful for the implementation of the Lin & Kernighan moves [FRE 95] as for the application of ejection chains [GAM 05]. These two techniques will be described in detail in section 5.3.

The two-level tree structure brings into play two concepts: segments and cities (Figure 5.1). A tour is divided up into approximately $\sqrt{n}$ segments. Each segment represents a chain of cities and its length is contained within the interval $\left[\dfrac{\sqrt{n}}{2}, 2\sqrt{n}\right]$. A segment carries with it these pieces of information:

– its identifier Id;

– its size, which represents the number of cities within the segment;

– a binary number, which specifies the direction of movement (0 forward, 1 backward);

– a pointer to the preceding segment;

– a pointer to the following segment;

– a pointer to the first city of the segment;

– a pointer to the last city of the segment.

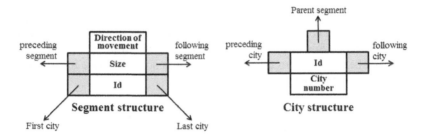

Figure 5.1. *Units of the two-level tree structures*

The city constitutes the second unit of this tree representation. A city belongs to a segment; hence, the term "two-level tree". The pieces of information provided by a city are:

– an identifier Id, which is used to identify the city within the segment it belongs to;

– a city number;

– a pointer to the segment it belongs to;

– a pointer to the city that will be visited before it;

– a pointer to the city that will be visited after it.

Figure 5.2 shows the coding for the permutation $\sigma = (3,6,5,7,2,1,8,4)$. We travel backwards along the third segment. Let us point out that in this kind of representation, the city identifiers within a segment follow one another but do not necessarily start at the value 1.

The significance of this type of coding lies in its ability to make changes to the permutations more quickly. We have seen for example that, in order to perform a two-opt move, we need to change the direction of movement along one of the two units created by removing the two edges. With a classic kind of coding we need to alter, on average, a quarter of the array elements (as long as we take care of inverting the direction of movement along the unit containing the smallest number of cities). The larger the number of cities, the more expensive the operation is. The two-level tree representation allows us to perform this operation in constant time (segment separation and union, update of some pointers and of the direction of movement). The experimental results reported in [GAM 05] show that the two representations are the same, in terms of execution time of the Lin & Kernighan heuristic, for problems dealing with 1,000 cities. The classic representation becomes around 4 times slower for problems dealing with 10,000 cities and around 50 times slower for problems with 100,000 cities.

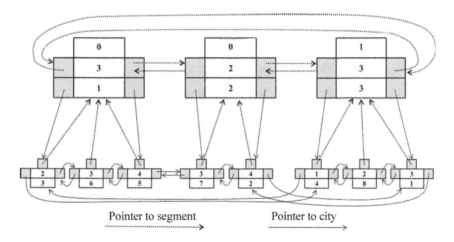

Pointer to segment

Pointer to city

Figure 5.2. *Coding for a permutation with a two-level tree structure*

5.2. Constructing initial solutions

Construction heuristics for the TSP are incredibly numerous. [REI 94] describes several of them and provides us with particularly well documented experimental results, showing clearly the strengths and weaknesses of each. We have chosen to focus on two heuristics: nearest neighbor search and the Christofides algorithm.

5.2.1. *A greedy heuristic: nearest neighbor*

The "Nearest Neighbor" (NN) [ROS 77] heuristic is certainly the method anyone would naturally employ if confronted for the first time with such a problem as the TSP. It is also a good approach to show how local optimal choices do not necessarily lead to an optimal solution or even, in some cases, to a good-quality tour. The core idea of this heuristic is the following: given a partial solution in the process of being constructed i.e. a subset of cities already visited and a current city, the traveling salesman will travel to the unvisited city closest to the current one. At first sight this heuristic is appealing. However, as the construction of the solution progresses, thus limiting the choice of cities yet to be visited accordingly, the traveling salesman will probably complete his route by traveling long distances between the last cities of his itinerary. This heuristic is shown in detail in Box 5.1. At each $n - 1$ iteration of the for loop, NN first of all searches for the unvisited closest city (*city_min*), then marks it and considers it as the next current city. In the variant considered here, this function returns the cost of the solution constructed. It is actually handy to calculate this cost as we proceed with the construction.

This heuristic offers numerous advantages:

– it is easily understandable and implementable;

– it quickly constructs a solution with an intrinsically average quality, which is however easily improvable;

– it enables us to generate several different solutions in relation to the city we chose as starting point (*city_init*);

– it is easily "randomizable" (by randomly choosing one of the closer cities, rather than the closest one).

// Construct a permutation σ and calculate the cost of the corresponding solution

Function $NN\ (\sigma : array, dist : array, city\_init : integer, n : integer)$

       Dim i, j : integer   \\ loop variables

       Dim *mark* : array   \\ marker of the visited cities

       Dim $city\_curr$: integer   \\ current city

       Dim $city\_min$, $dmin$: integer   \\ closest city and its distance

       Dim *cost* : integer   \\ sum of the distances

       For i **from** 1 **to** n **Do**

              $mark(i) = 0$

       End For

       $mark(city\_init) = 1$

       $\cos t = 0$

       $city\_curr = city\_init$

       $\sigma(1) = city\_init$

       For i **from** 2 **to** n **Do**

            \\ search for the unvisited city closest to $city\_curr$

            $city\_min = -1$

            $dmin = +\infty$

            For j **from** 1 **to** n **Do**

                 If $mark(j) = 0$ **and** $dist(city\_curr, j) < dmin$ **Then**

                     $dmin = dist(city\_curr, j)$

                     $city\_min = j$

                 End If

            End For

            \\ update

            $cost = cost + dmin$

            $city\_curr = city\_min$

            $Mark(city\_min) = 1$

            $\sigma(i) = city\_min$

       End For

       Return $cost = cost + dist(city\_curr, city\_init)$

End Function

Box 5.1. *Detailed algorithm of the NN heuristic*

5.2.2. A simplification heuristic: the Christofides algorithm

In Chapter 2 we described the TSP as an extension of the assignment problem (which is polynomial) in which any sub-cycle is prohibited. The TSP may equally be seen as an extension of the minimum-cost spanning tree problem (section 2.2.3) in which we require the degree of each vertex to be equal to two. The Christofides algorithm [CHR 76] is a four-stage heuristic that exploits this link between the two problems. Box 5.2 shows these stages.

\\ stages of Christofides' heuristic procedure
Stage 1: Solve the minimum-cost spanning tree problem
Stage 2: Construct a Eulerian path from the spanning tree
Stage 3: Construct a Eulerian cycle
Stage 4: Construct a Hamiltonian cycle : Christofides tour

Box 5.2. *Basic form of the Christofides algorithm*

Let us give a more detailed description of these stages:

− stage 1 consists of applying Prim or Kruskal's algorithm, thanks to which we obtain a minimum-cost spanning tree in polynomial time;

− this spanning tree has an even number of vertices with an odd degree (the sum of the degrees of all vertices clearly being even). A necessary and sufficient condition for a connected graph to be Eulerian is that each vertex has an even degree (Euler-Hierholzer theorem). By adding to the spanning tree some edges between the vertices with an odd degree, we will obtain a Eulerian path. These vertices can be added by solving the minimum cost perfect matching problem (which can in turn be solved in $O(n^3)$ with Edmonds' algorithm [EDM 65]). Other variants simply advise doubling the edges of the spanning tree;

− stage 3 consists of constructing a Eulerian cycle from this graph. This can be done thanks to Euler's algorithm (Box 5.5), which proposes a recursive construction. A vertex is called isolated when, in the graph, no edge is incident to it. This condition is the basis for recursion. Then the function returns this vertex. Otherwise, the function returns a cycle constructed from the vertex that now constitutes the parameter;

− stage 4 consists of constructing a Hamiltonian cycle from the Eulerian one by means of a simple read-out and a removal of those vertices that recur more than once (duplicates).

// Construct a Eulerian cycle from a Eulerian path $G = (X, E)$

Function *Euler* $(G : graph, x : integer)$: list

    Dim ϕ : list   \\ list of the vertices visited

    Dim y, z : integer   \\ variables of the vertex tour

    Dim k : integer

    $\phi \leftarrow [x]$ \\ initialization

    $k \leftarrow 1$

    If x is an isolated vertex **then**

        Return ϕ

    Else

        $y \leftarrow x$

        While y is not an isolated vertex **Do**

            Choose $z / (y, z) \in E$

            $E \leftarrow E \setminus \{(y, z)\}$ \\ the edge is removed

            $\phi \leftarrow \phi \circ [y]$ \\ the vertex y is added to the cycle

            $k \leftarrow k + 1$

        End While

        Return *Euler* $(G, \phi(1)) \circ \ldots \circ$ *Euler* $(G, \phi(k))$

    End If

End Function

Box 5.3. *Euler's algorithm for the construction of a Eulerian cycle*

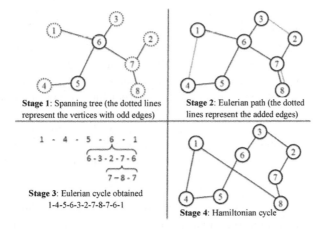

Stage 1: Spanning tree (the dotted lines represent the vertices with odd edges)

Stage 2: Eulerian path (the dotted lines represent the added edges)

$$1 - 4 - 5 - 6 - 1$$
$$6 - 3 - 2 - 7 - 6$$
$$7 - 8 - 7$$

Stage 3: Eulerian cycle obtained
1-4-5-6-3-2-7-8-7-6-1

Stage 4: Hamiltonian cycle

Figure 5.3. *The four stages of the construction of the Christofides algorithm*

The stages of the construction of the Christofides algorithm are displayed in Figure 5.3. As for the application of Euler's algorithm in stage 3, we conventionally choose the vertex z with the smallest index. The Christofides algorithm is a singular heuristic. Unlike many others, it is not very intuitive. Furthermore, it is hard to implement since the first three stages require the application of a specific algorithm (the last stage does not require any particular effort). What is more, the solution obtained is often of rather mediocre quality. Because of all these shortcomings, we may pay little attention to it. However, many regard it as an excellent starting point for some improving procedures. The general structure of a tour constructed with this heuristic is globally quite good and allows us to focus the search on very interesting areas of the search space.

After discussing construction heuristics, we will now present two neighborhood systems effective in the search for good-quality solutions.

5.3. Neighborhood systems

The simple moves we introduced in the previous section (exchange, insertion, inversion, etc.) can only modify a solution very slightly. The neighborhoods to be examined are limited but on the other hand the local minima associated with them are numerous and not necessarily all of good quality.

The notion of large-scale neighborhood can compensate for this. In absolute terms, if each element of the search space is in the neighborhood of a solution, then the global optimum is also necessarily situated within it. The idea is then to devise some neighborhoods that will allow us to make more significant changes aimed to provide local minima of good quality. The simplest example is the k-opt neighborhood for the TSP. These neighborhoods consist of removing k edges from the current solution and reconnecting the parts to reconstruct a Hamiltonian cycle. The two-opt neighborhood corresponds to the inversion move we have already described (Box 4.4). k-opt neighborhoods are nested neighborhoods (k-opt is included in $(k + 1)$-opt) and clearly, if $k = n$, any two solutions are neighbors with each other.

The concept of large-scale neighborhood is then quite appealing but the price to pay is calculation time that quickly increases too much to justify a classic neighborhood exploration. Setting up guidance techniques enables us to be more aggressive in the search for good solutions. The idea that we are going to develop in this chapter is known as variable depth search. It consists of progressively and dynamically increasing the value of k by directing the search from one level to the next one. First we will introduce the Lin & Kernighan operation, which is groundbreaking in this field, and then we will describe the works on ejection chains, which may be regarded as a generalization of the Lin & Kernighan operations.

5.3.1. *The Lin & Kernighan neighborhood*

This neighborhood is only applied to the symmetric TSP, in which the cost necessary to go from one city to another does not depend on the direction of the itinerary.

More than 40 years ago, Lin & Kernighan [LIN 73] put forward a pioneering neighborhood strategy, which is still relevant nowadays. The aim was to generalize the two-opt and three-opt moves which, despite having already obtained good results, were constrained by the fixed number of edges (or arcs) removed. The designers started from this observation. A non-optimal solution T differs from an optimal solution T^* by an integer k and by the edges $x_1,\ldots,x_k \in T$, which need to be replaced by the edges $y_1,\ldots,y_k \notin T$. The difficulties involved in making the tour T optimal consist of the identification of this number k as well as of the edges $x_1,\ldots,x_k$ and $y_1,\ldots,y_k$. The idea is to try to determine these elements progressively by starting with a first pair of edges (x_1,y_1), located in the worst position possible, then moving on to a second pair (x_2,y_2), etc.

For that reason, the designers introduced the notion of sequential transformation. It is possible to sequentially transform a solution T into a solution T' if we can number the removed edges $x_1,\ldots,x_k$ and the added edges $y_1,\ldots,y_k$ so that the edges x_i and y_i share a vertex, as well as the edges y_i and x_{i+1} (by setting down $x_{k+1} = x_1$). We will then be able to show a sequence of vertices $(t_1,\ldots,t_{2k})$ that satisfies $x_i = (t_{2i-1},t_{2i})$ and $y_i = (t_{2i},t_{2i+1})$ for any $i = 1,\ldots,k$.

Let us illustrate our point with an example (Figure 5.4). Let $T = [1,2,3,4,5,6,7,8]$ be the initial solution (Figure 5.4(a)). Let us suppose that we start with city $t_1 = 1$ and that we decide to remove the edge $x_1 = (1,2)$. City two becomes the current city, i.e. the starting point from which we have to add another edge, for example $y_1 = (2,5)$ (Figure 5.4(b)). The current city is now city five. By adding this edge we have introduced a cycle, in this case the cycle $[2,3,4,5]$ that we should disrupt. This is why the next edge to be removed is the edge $x_2 = (5,4)$, which is the only choice allowed. From city four onwards, it is possible to construct a feasible solution by returning to the starting city through the addition of the edge $(4,1)$. We have performed a two-opt move (Figure 5.4(c)). Let us suppose that this solution is not satisfactory and that we add the edge $y_2 = (4,7)$ in its stead. The disruption of the cycle $[7,6,5,2,3,4,7]$ leads us then to remove the edge $x_3 = (7,6)$. By linking the current city to the starting city $y_3 = (6,1)$, we have constructed another solution, which is a three-opt move (Figure 5.4(d)). We suppose that the solution we have obtained for this example is satisfactory (its cost is better than that of the initial solution) and we terminate the move at this stage. The sequence of vertices is then $(t_1, \ldots, t_6) = (1,2,5,4,7,6)$.

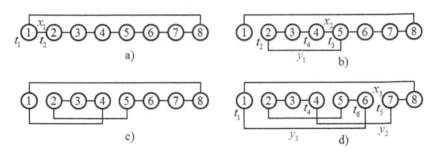

Figure 5.4. *An example of a 3-opt sequential move*

Thus, the LK move tries to construct a sequential transformation of one solution into another one. Before moving on, we should point out that it is not always possible to find a sequential transformation of one solution into another. The "double-bridge" move, which is a particular four-opt move (see Figure 5.5), is a famous counterexample of that. The consequence is that the double-bridge is a very efficient exploration move (for instance to perturb a solution) when the neighborhood used to explore (a local search for example) generates sequential moves.

The second strong point of the algorithm consists of the clever application of an arithmetic property that is not very well-known, which is formulated as follows:

PROPERTY.– Given a sequence of numbers $(g_1,...,g_n)$ whose sum is strictly positive, there must be a cyclic permutation of these numbers such that all partial sums are strictly positive.

PROOF.– Let k be the largest index such that $g_1 +...+ g_{k-1}$ is minimal. Then the cyclic permutation $(g_k,...,g_n,g_1,...,g_{k-1})$ satisfies the desired condition. In fact:

If $k \le i \le n$, then $g_k +...+ g_i = (g_1 +...+ g_i)-(g_1 +...+ g_{k-1}) > 0$

If $1 \le i < k$, then $g_k +...+ g_n + g_1 +...+ g_i \ge g_k +...+ g_n +(g_1 +...+ g_{k-1}) > 0$

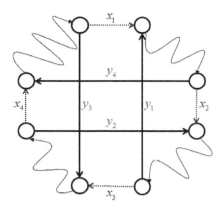

Figure 5.5. *A non-sequential move: the double bridge*

Let us remember that we are aiming to exchange sequentially the pairs of edges so that one solution T is transformed into an improved solution T' or, in other words, the profit $G = H(T)-H(T') > 0$. If we set down $g_i = |x_i|-|y_i|$, where $|x_i|$ is the length of the edge x_i, then $G = \sum_{i=1}^{k} g_i$. In more concrete terms, this means that if there is a sequential transformation that can improve a solution, then we will only be able to search for the sequence of edges that ensures a constantly positive partial gain with no restrictions. This tool allows us to guide the search for an improving solution very effectively.

The basic Lin & Kernighan algorithm is shown in Box 5.4.

// Lin & Kernighan construction of an improving solution
Stage 1: Generate an initial solution
Stage 2: Choose a starting city t_1 and an incident edge $x_1 = (t_1, t_2)$

$\quad\quad i \leftarrow 1$
$\quad\quad G^* \leftarrow 0 \quad\quad\quad$ \\ maximum gain
Stage 3: Choose $y_1 = (t_2, t_3)$ with $g_1 > 0$. If no y_1 is suitable then go to stage 5
Stage 4: $i \leftarrow i+1$
Choose $x_i = (t_{2i-1}, t_{2i})$ and $y_i = (t_{2i}, t_{2i+1})$ as follows

a) x_i is determined uniquely in such a way that by linking t_{2i} to t_1 we can reconstruct a feasible solution.

b) y_i is chosen so that we can satisfy the constraints 4c, 4d and 4e. If no y_i is suitable, then go to stage 5.

c) To make sure that the x_i and y_i elements are unconnected, x_i cannot be a previously added edge and y_i cannot be a previously removed edge.

d) $G_i = \sum_{j=1}^{i} g_j > 0$ (partial gain must be always positive)

e) the chosen y_i element must remain feasible at the iteration $i+1$. We have to be able to remove the edge x_{i+1}.

f) Before choosing y_i we have to verify that we do not gain more by completing the tour with the edge (t_{2i}, t_1). Let $y_i^* = (t_{2i}, t_1)$ and $g_i^* = |y_i^*| - |x_i|$.

If $G_{i-1} + g_i^* > G^*$ then $G^* \leftarrow G_{i-1} + g_i^*$ and $k \leftarrow i$ (k lets us find the edges to be exchanged that led to the improvement G^*)
Stage 5:
If $G^* > 0$ then we construct the corresponding solution by performing
$S \leftarrow S \cup \{x_1, \ldots, x_k\} \setminus \{y_1, \ldots, y_k\}$

Box 5.4. *Basic algorithm of the LK move*

The heuristic procedures based on the LK moves are some of the most impressive when used on the symmetric TSP. [HEL 00] proposed several improvements. The resulting heuristic, called LKH, is regarded as one of the most effective nowadays. It has broken all records for the "DIMACS TSP CHALLENGE" library [DIM 00], which consists of cases from 10,000 to 10,000,000 cities.

5.3.2. *Ejection chain techniques*

Ejection chains belong to this category of neighborhoods, which can substantially modify a solution in order to improve it by effectively guiding the exploration of the search space. They have been successfully applied to several combinatorial optimization problems, among which the TSP [GLO 92, REG 98]. These are the studies we are now describing in detail.

The designers we mentioned describe an ejection chain procedure based on edges. This method relies on a basic structure called "Stem-and-Cycle", which is illustrated in Figure 5.6. A "Stem-and-Cycle" is a spanning tree of n edges consisting of two parts: the stem and the cycle. The stem is a path $ST = (t,...,r)$ linking the tip of the stem t to the cycle. The vertex shared by the stem and the cycle is called the root r. The two vertices of the cycle adjacent to the root are called sub-root 1 (s_1) and sub-root 2 (s_2). The cycle can be thus written as $CY = (r, s_1,...,s_2, r)$. In the specific case of $r = t$, the stem is said to be degenerate and the structure corresponds then to a Hamiltonian cycle or, in other words, to a feasible solution of the TSP.

Starting from a non-degenerate "Stem-and-Cycle", it is easy to reconstruct two cycles by adding one of the edges (t, s_i) and removing the edge (r, s_i) for $i = 1, 2$. These cycles are also shown in Figure 5.6.

The designers turn one "Stem-and-Cycle" into another by adding another edge that links the tip t (the only vertex of the tree with degree 1) to another vertex p. Then they set two rules according to which p belongs to either the stem or the cycle. The application of these rules is shown in Figure 5.7.

Rule 1: Add an edge (t, p) with $p \in CY$. We then remove one of the two edges incident to p. Let (p, q) be this edge. We obtain a new "Stem-and-

Cycle" with $ST=(q,...,r)$, while q becomes the new tip. Let us point out that, if $q=r$, the stem is degenerate.

Rule 2: Add an edge (t,p) with $p \in ST$. The edge (p,q) is removed, q – the vertex adjacent to p – being situated on the path $(t,...,p)$. In the new structure we have obtained, q becomes again the tip of the stem $(q,...,r)$.

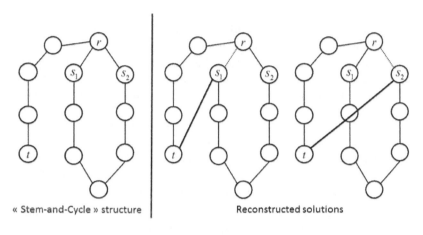

« Stem-and-Cycle » structure   Reconstructed solutions

Figure 5.6. *"Stem-and-Cycle" structure and corresponding solutions*

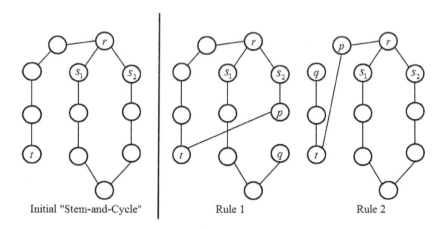

Initial "Stem-and-Cycle"   Rule 1   Rule 2

Figure 5.7. *Changes to "Stem-and-Cycle" structures*

By applying in succession rules 1 and 2, we construct a sequence of structures $(SC_1, SC_2, ..., SC_k)$ in which we go from SC_i to SC_{i+1} $(i = 1, ..., k-1)$ by changing a pair of edges. This constitutes a marked similarity between ejection chains and the Lin & Kernighan move, all the more so since in both cases the move performed is sequential. The designers differ in relation to the constraints they have used in order to avoid generating structures that reconstruct solutions that have already been considered. The removed edges become tabu and can no longer be added. On the contrary, the edges that have been added can always be removed. If such a case arises, the edge that will be added immediately afterwards will no longer be removable. These restrictions are managed by two lists of tabu edges: a list of those that can no longer be added and a list of those that can no longer be removed.

The authors then define the legitimate neighborhood of a city v as the set of closest cities to v that abide by the restrictions of the tabu list. This component can curb exploration by considering only, at any moment, the cities that are closest to the current one. The added edges are, thus, those that cost little.

In Box 5.5 we show the basic algorithm of these ejection chains. We define as p^- and p^+ the preceding and following city, respectively, of the city p for a given direction.

// Modify the solution S starting from the city r with an l-level ejection chain

Procedure $EjectlonChain(S : array, l : integer, r : integer)$

$tip \leftarrow r$

$k \leftarrow 0$, $k^* \leftarrow 0$

$SC \leftarrow [r]$

$\Delta^* = -\infty$

While $LN(tip) \neq \emptyset$ and $k < l$ **Do**

    \\ Assessment of the ejection chain

    For each city $p \in LN(tip)$ **Do**

        If $p \in ST$ **then**   (rule 2)

            Identify $q \leftarrow p^-$ or $q \leftarrow p^+$ accordingly

            $g = d(tip, p) - d(p, q)$

Else   (rule 1)
$$g = d(tip, p) - \max\left[d(p, p^-), d(p, p^+) \right]$$

End If

End For

Choose the cities p^* and q^* that minimize the value of g

Verify the solution reconstruction cost

$$\Delta = g + \min_{i=1,2}\left[d(q^*, s_i) - d(s_i, r) \right]$$

If $\Delta > \Delta^*$ **then**

$$\Delta^* = \Delta$$
$$k^* = k$$

End If

Update the tabu list

$k \leftarrow k + 1$

$tip \leftarrow q^*$

$SC \leftarrow SC \oplus\left[(p^*, q^*) \right]$

End While

Update the solution S with SC and k^*

Box 5.5. *Basic algorithm of the ejection chain*

Let us point out that [GAM 05] implemented this ejection chain method with the two-level tree structure to deal with problems involving very large quantities (up to 100,000 cities).

5.4. Some results

In Table 5.1 we propose first a comparison between 11 cases of the TSP, which are available on the TSPLIB [REI 91]. The number included in the case name corresponds to the number of cities. The cost of the optimal solution is shown in the column "*Optimal*". For each procedure, the value given is the difference in relation to the optimal solution. If x is the solution provided by a procedure and x^* an optimal solution, this difference is calculated by means of the formula $100 \times \dfrac{H(x) - H(x^*)}{H(x^*)}$. We show the results obtained by means of the nearest neighbor heuristic (column "NN"), the Christofides algorithm (column "Christofides"), a two-opt neighborhood local search (column "LS"), a two-opt neighborhood iterated local search with the Better acceptance criterion and a calculation time of 30 seconds (column "ILS (2-opt)"), and the same iterated local search with a Lin & Kernighan neighborhood system (column "ILS (LK)"). The results of the first three methods are drawn from [REI 94]. We have obtained the ILS results through our own work.

The results of local search represent the average of 1,000 local minima obtained by starting from a random permutation generated through the Fisher–Yates algorithm. Those of iterated local search represent the average of 10 replications (10 executions that modify only the random generator source).

These results represent what we can typically obtain with other problems. There is a marked hierarchy between construction heuristics, which are quite far from an optimal solution (around 20%) when dealing with substantial sizes. The local search method hovers around 8%. With a standard metaheuristic (the one implemented with the knowledge acquired in the previous chapter) we get to around 1% of an optimal solution. Employing LK moves actually enables us to outclass the previous results (on average we get to less than 0.2% for the set of cases).

Instance	Optimal	NN	Christofides	LS	ILS (2-OPT)	ILS (LK)
D198	15780	25,79	15,67	3,18	0,10	0,00
LIN318	42028	26,85	18,42	5,94	0,11	0,02
FL417	11861	21,28	24,52	7,25	0,93	0,02
PCB442	50778	21,36	18,59	7,82	0,07	0,07
U574	36905	29,60	20,08	7,02	0,95	0,26
P654	34643	31,02	21,73	12,37	1,25	0,03
RAT783	8806	27,13	21,34	8,39	1,46	0,25
PR1002	259045	24,35	20,67	8,48	1,61	0,38
U1060	224094	30,43	18,97	9,11	1,35	0,37
PCB1173	56892	28,18	18,77	9,42	1,40	0,34
D1291	50801	22,97	24,31	9,62	1,04	0,29
Average		26,27	20,28	8,05	0,93	0,18

Table 5.1. *Some results for the TSP*

5.5. Conclusion

Let us review this chapter. We have seen that in order to improve the effectiveness of metaheuristics – in comparison with the standard implementation advanced in Chapter 4 – we need to add some other components that can introduce problem-specific knowledge into them. We have highlighted several methods to improve the TSP:

– choosing a more sophisticated representation of the solutions, able to manipulate more effectively cases involving very large sizes;

– defining a construction heuristic, the Christofides algorithm, which provides us with an excellent initial solution for iterative improvement methods, which metaheuristics belong to;

– employing the "double-bridge" move, which is non-sequential, as a tool for perturbing the solution;

– using variable depth neighborhoods that can effectively exploit the knowledge acquired in the search space.

In the next chapter we proceed to show how these ideas can be applied to the permutation flow-shop problem.

6

The Flow-Shop Problem

The permutation flow-shop scheduling problem (FSSP) is one of the scheduling problems that receives the most attention from the scientific literature. With a fully-stacked and well-documented library of cases, it is an ideal problem, like that of the traveling salesman, for those who want to test new ideas.

I had the opportunity, in the course of my research activities, to adapt the ejection-chain ideas to this problem. It is this experience, which helped me to acquire very good results, even though it was not widely published and remains poorly known, that I would like to share in this chapter.

The flow-shop problem is presented in section 2.5.1.

6.1. Representation and assessment of a solution

The permutation flow-shop problem is characterized by the order in which parts enter the workshop, and that order remains the same for all machines. It is, therefore, natural to represent a solution by a permutation. The flow-shop includes many different solutions as there are permutations; namely $n!$ if n is the number of parts.

To assess this solution, we assume that an operation starts as soon as all conditions necessary for its execution are met. Schedules built this way are called semi-active. It is not possible to move forward with the execution of an operation without calling into question the order of parts of machines. This assumption is not restrictive at all because it was shown that at least an optimum solution exists among all semi-active schedules. It is this solution which will be the focus of our work.

Let us remember that I refers to all the n parts and J to all the m machines. The processing time of part i on machine j is noted $p_{i,j}$. Let $t_{i,j}$ be the completion time for part i on machine j. Function makespan in Box 6.1 computes, for a given permutation σ, the time $t_{\sigma(i),j}$ for every $1 \le i \le n$ and $1 \le j \le m$. By taking as initial time the date of entry of the first part $\sigma(1)$ on the first machine, we obtain $t_{\sigma(1),1} = p_{\sigma(1),1}$. This allows us to compute the processing time on the first machine (loop for $i \in \{2,...,n\}$) and for the first part (loop for $j \in \{2,...,m\}$). Every other operation (double loop for $i \in \{2,...,n\}$, $j \in \{2,...,m\}$) cannot start until part i has finished its processing on the previous machine $t_{\sigma(i),j-1}$ and until machine j finishes processing of the previous part $t_{\sigma(i-1),j}$. The function returns the makespan (process completion time for the last part $\sigma(n)$ on machine m. Once the process finishing timetable is completed, it is possible to calculate criteria other than the makespan.

6.2. Construction of the initial solution

We propose two very classical heuristics to construct the initial solution; their names correspond to the initials of the authors who introduced them: CDS and NEH. The first one is a simplification heuristic and the second one is a greedy heuristic.

```
// determine the makespan for permutation σ
Function makespan (σ : array, p : array, m : integer, n : integer)
        Dim i, j : integer
        Dim t : array
        t_σ(1),1 = p_σ(1),1
        // Calculation of completion time on first machine
        For i from 2 to n Do
                t_σ(i),1 = t_σ(i-1),1 + p_σ(i),1
        End For
        // Calculation of completion time for first piece
```

For i from 2 to m **Do**
$$t_{\sigma(1),j} = t_{\sigma(1),j-1} + p_{\sigma(1),j}$$
End **For**
//Calculation of completion time for any given operation
For i from 2 to n **Do**
For j from 2 to m **Do**
$$t_{\sigma(i),j} = \max\left(t_{\sigma(i-1),j}, t_{\sigma(i),j-1}\right) + p_{\sigma(i),j}$$
End For
End For
Return $t_{\sigma(n),m}$ // makespan

End Function

Box 6.1. *Calculation of completion time*

6.2.1. *Simplification heuristics: CDS*

[CAM 70] proposes a heuristic called CDS that leans on the two-machine flow-shop to find a solution to the general problem on m machine. We begin by introducing the two-machine flow-shop before turning to the CDS heuristic.

6.2.1.1. *The two-machine flow-shop*

The problem of the two-machine flow-shop, with the makespan criterion, is a polynomial problem. [JOH 54] provides a rule which allows constructing an optimal solution. This rule states that piece i_1 precedes piece i_2 in an optimal solution if $\min\left(p_{i_1,1}, p_{i_2,2}\right) < \min\left(p_{i_1,2}, p_{i_2,1}\right)$.

The *Johnson* function shown in Box 6.2 enables us to prepare a scheduling which satisfies the Johnson rule, and that is therefore optimal.

When considering the example of Table 6.1, the partition of parts that is obtained is $U = \{2, 4, 6, 8, 10, 12\}$ and $V = \{1, 3, 5, 7, 9, 11\}$. The sorting of both sets gives the sequences $[4, 6, 8, 10, 12, 2]$ for U and $[3, 5, 9, 11, 7, 1]$ for V. Concatenation of both sequences gives us the scheduling $\sigma = [4, 6, 8, 10, 12, 2, 3, 5, 9, 11, 7, 1]$ which is optimal (we propose as an exercise to create the Gantt chart linked to this resolution and to prove that the value of the makespan is of 128).

```
// Prepare an optimal scheduling for the two-machine flow-shop
Function Johnson (p : array, n : integer)

        Dim U,V : array

        Construct U = {i ∈ I / p_{i,1} < p_{i,2}}

        Construct V = {i ∈ I / p_{i,1} ≥ p_{i,2}}

        Sort out U according to the values of p_{i,1} in ascending order

        Sort out V according to the values of p_{i,2} in decreasing order

        Return the concatenation of U and V
End Function
```

Box 6.2. *Calculation of process finishing time*

Parts	1	2	3	4	5	6	7	8	9	10	11	12
Machine 1	7	12	10	7	10	8	15	9	11	10	10	11
Machine 2	6	14	9	12	9	9	8	10	9	13	9	13

Table 6.1. *Example of a two-machine flow shop*

6.2.1.2. *Principle of CDS heuristics*

The principle of CDS heuristics is very simple. m machines are separated into two groups; each group is made up of successive machines. There are $m-1$ possibilities of constructing such groupings. For instance, with $m = 3$ we have two possibilities. The first group of machines can be made up of a single machine, or machines one and two. The second group has the remaining machine(s). By assessing operating lengths on these groups, the flow-shop comes down to a two-machine problem in which Johnson's algorithm is applied. [CAM 70] proposes to take the sum of the processing times of the machines on each group. Nothing forbids one taking the mean, which has the advantage of providing more homogeneous values on both groups.

A detailed CDS pseudocode is shown in Box 6.3. This heuristic allows $m-1$ different scheduling to be constructed. The one which minimizes the makespan is kept.

Figure 6.1 shows the full functioning of the heuristic. The example with three machines and seven parts that appeared in Chapter 2 is shown again at the top of the figure. The rest of the figure is vertically separated into two parts according to the machine groups that can be established. To the left, the first group is composed of a single machine. To the right, the first group is composed of machines 1 and 2. The operating lengths on each of the groups are assessed by taking the average of the corresponding processing times, as explained previously. The Johnson algorithm is then applied. We show subsets U and V already sorted out. Concatenation $U \oplus V$ forms a scheduling that is evaluated on the Gantt chart. We obtain two makespan solutions: 67 and 69, respectively. The chosen solution is then $\sigma = [5, 7, 6, 3, 1, 4, 2]$ with a makespan equal to 67.

```
// Heurestic
Function CDS (p : array, m : integer, n : integer)
        Dim σ, σ_rec : array           // one solution and solution record
        Dim H, H_rec : integer         // one makespan and the makespan record
        Dim p̄ : array                  // operating lengths on the machine groups
        Dim i, k : integer             // loop variables
        H_rec ← +∞
        For k from 1 to m−1 Do
        // namely, the machine groups G₁ = {1,...,k} and G₁ = {k+1,...,m}
                For i from 1 to n Do
```
$$\overline{p_{i,1}} = \frac{1}{k}\sum_{j=1}^{k} p_{i,j}$$

$$\overline{p_{i,2}} = \frac{1}{m-k}\sum_{j=k+1}^{m} p_{i,j}$$

```
                End for
                σ = johnson(p̄, n)
                H_rec ← makespan(σ, p, m, n)
                If H < H_rec Then
                        H_rec ← H
                        σ_rec ← σ
                End If
        End For
        Return σ_rec
End Function
```

Box 6.3. *Algorithm of the CDS principle*

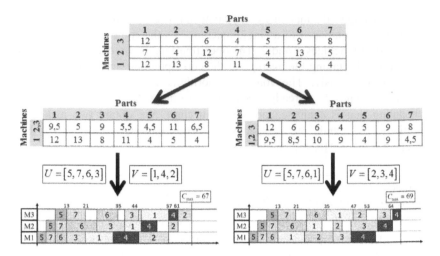

Figure 6.1. *Illustration of how the CDS heuristic works*

6.2.2. *A greedy heuristic: NEH*

[NAW 83] imagined a heuristic in two stages, a stage of sorting and a stage of construction, which allows for the construction of a solution progressively. This heuristic is still considered today by many to be one of the best constructing methods for the flow-shop problem. It is widely used to provide the initial solution for other methods, especially for metaheuristics. The full functioning of NEH is shown in Figure 6.2.

The sort stage consists of arranging the parts according to the sum of their processing times in decreasing order. In other words, from the most expensive to the least expensive of all in terms of manufacturing costs. Taking the previous example, the manufacturing period of piece 1 is 12+7+12=31. It is the most expensive piece as we can see in the figure. By computing the other durations, we obtain the arrangement $[1,6,3,2,4,7,5]$.

The construction stage consists, starting from the partial solution formed only by the costliest piece (on the example of piece 1), of inserting one piece after the other according to the order defined during the sort stage. Each piece is inserted in the position where makespan is minimized. On our example, piece 6 is inserted before piece 1, since partial solution 6–1 has a 39 makespan, as compared to 41 for partial solution 1–6. Then, piece 3 is inserted in the 6–1 arrangement by choosing the best position among solutions 3–6–1, 6–3–1 and 6–1–3. The best positions appear shaded and in bold in the figure. It is, therefore, solution 6–1–3 which will be kept and that will act as a basis afterwards. By developing the heuristic until the end, one obtains the solution 5–7–6–1–3–4–2 for which the Gantt chart is created. We can point out that the solution acquired with NEH is very similar to that acquired with CDS. Both solutions have the same makespan and differ from one another by a simple exchange between parts 1 and 3. This is due to the fact that we present these two methods with an example of very small size. In cases of bigger size, NEH usually provides solutions of much better quality.

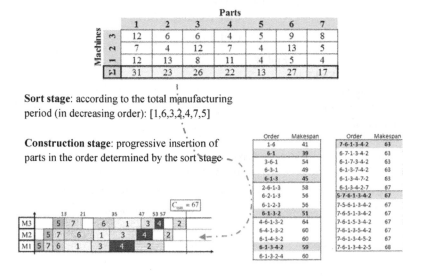

Figure 6.2. *Illustration of how the NEH heuristic works*

A detailed NEH pseudocode is shown in Box 6.4. Function NEH makes use of two functions corresponding to each phase of the heuristics. Furthermore, this code makes use of procedures *Exchange* (Box 6.2) and *Insertion* (Figure 6.2), described in Chapter 4.

```
// Create liste of parts, sorted out according to the manufacturing period
Function NEH _ sort (p : array, m : integer, n : integer)

        Dim list : array          // list of parts
        Dim df  : array          // manufacturing period of the parts
        Dim i , j : integer  // loop variables
        // initialization of arrays
```

For i **from** 1 **to** n **Do**

$$list[i] \leftarrow i$$

$$df[i] \leftarrow \sum_{j=1}^{m} p_{i,j}$$

End For

// sorting of the board *list*

For i **from** 1 **to** $n-1$ **Do**

For j **from** $i+1$ **to** n **Do**

If $df[i] < df[j]$ **Then**

Call $Exchange(list, i, j)$

Call $Exchange(df, i, j)$

End If

End For

End For

Return *list*

End Function

\\ create a solution by inserting parts progressively

Function $NEH\_Construction(p : array, list : array, m : integer, n : integer)$

Dim pos, pos_{min} : integer   // current insertion position and record

Dim H, H_{min} : integer   // cost of current solution and record

Dim σ : array   // solution to be determined

Dim k : integer   // loop variable

$\sigma[1] \leftarrow list[1]$

For k **from** 2 **to** n **Do**   // insertion of the kth piece

$\sigma[k] \leftarrow list[k]$

$pos_{min} \leftarrow k$

$H_{min} \leftarrow makespan(\sigma, p, m, k)$

For pos **from** k -1 **to** 1 **for** -1 **Do**

Call $Exchange(\sigma, pos, pos+1)$

$H \leftarrow makespan(\sigma, p, m, k)$

If $H < H_{min}$ **Then**

$H_{min} \leftarrow H$

$pos_{min} \leftarrow pos$

End If

```
                    End For
                    Call  Insertion(σ,1, pos_min)

              End For
              Return  σ
        End Function

        //  NEH Heuristic
        Function NEH (p : array, m : integer, n : integer)
              Dim list : array              // list of parts

                 list ← NEH _ sort(p,m,n)
                 Return  NEH _ construction(p,list,m,n)
        End Function
```

Box 6.4. *Algorithm of the NEH principle*

The role of the first stage is, at the start of construction, to arrange parts according to their cost. The least expensive parts are kept for the end. They are better suited for integrating to the partial scheduling without unsettling it much. However, nothing prevents one from applying the construction stage with a different sequence; for instance, with a sequence generated randomly by the Fisher–Yates shuffle (section 4.2.1). NEH therefore allows creating many schedulings. This heuristic can be used to generate an initial population in the framework of a population-based metaheuristics. The only negative point is the risk of generating an initial population that is made up by similar solutions (since they are generated from the same construction mechanism), and that it is not accurately spread in the search space.

6.3. Neighborhood systems

As solutions are represented by a permutation, classic neighborhood systems on this type of representation (insertion, exchange and inversion) are commonly used. In the context of the overall scheduling problems, and of flow-shop specifically, inversion between two parts is a movement that does not work well. The reason for this is that one piece can perfectly fit after another, without being necessarily the same case the other way around. Figure 6.3 shows a sequence of parts [7–4–2–1] whose operations link up perfectly; that is clearly not the case for the reverse sequence [1–2–4–7]. This non-symmetry indicates that the assessments of a sequence of parts in one direction or the other have no reason to be correlated, which is detrimental to the proper functioning of methods that would lean on this neighborhood.

Figure 6.3. *Setbacks of the inversion movement*

[TAI 90] proposed in principle what is an improvement of the NEH heuristic, but also helps to improve the efficiency of the insertion movement and is, therefore, useful for every neighborhood method. We present those works in section 6.3.1, before elaborating on them in section 6.3.2.

6.3.1. *Improvement of the insertion movements*

The algorithm proposed by [TAI 90] allows us to determine the best position to insert a piece (designated with index n) in a partial solution of $n-1$ parts. In our version of Taillard's algorithm (Box 6.8), we consider a permutation $\sigma = (\sigma_1, \sigma_2, ..., \sigma_n)$ and we try to insert the last piece $\sigma_n = n$ in a partial solution made up by the $n-1$ first parts $\overline{\sigma} = (\sigma_1, \sigma_2, ..., \sigma_{n-1})$. Taillard's algorithm allows us to calculate the n makespans M_i that are obtained when inserting piece σ_n into the ith position ($1 \le i \le n$) in $\overline{\sigma}$, with an algorithm complexity comparable to the evaluation of a single makespan. The evaluation of makespans M_i needs to determine three elements beforehand:

– Compute the earliest completion time $e_{i,j}$ of the ith job (σ_i) on the jth machine for $1 \le i \le n-1$ and $1 \le j \le m$. This calculation is identical to that performed to determine the makespan. A fictitious line $i = 0$ and a fictitious column $j = 0$ are added to integrate the calculation of all the $e_{i,j}$ in the same loop.

– Compute the tail $q_{i,j}$, which represents the minimal distance between the start of the piece's manufacturing σ_i on the machine j and the end of the project (makespan) when all the tasks are put off (placed to the right on a Gantt chart). The partial solution always includes $n-1$ parts for this calculation, which explains loops $1 \le i \le n-1$ and $1 \le j \le m$. The mechanism of this calculation is identical to that of the makespan, except that it is performed in reverse, starting from the end.

– Compute the earliest relative completion time $f_{i,j}$ the piece σ_n on the jth machine of job is inserted at the ith position. The solution obtained after the insertion of this piece now includes n parts. The calculation is, therefore, performed for $1 \le i \le n$ and $1 \le j \le m$. The formula is similar to the calculation of the makespan, except that one must take the max between $f_{i,j-1}$ and $e_{i-1,j}$ with $f_{i,j-1}$ the completion time of the piece σ_n on the preceding machine $j-1$ and $e_{i-1,j}$ the completion time of the piece σ_{i-1} on the current machine j. It is important to add to this result the processing time $p_{\sigma_n,j}$ of the piece n on the machine j.

// Taillard implementation – effective insertion of one piece
Function *Insertion_Taillard* $(\sigma : array, p : array, m : integer, n : integer)$

    Dim e : array   // date of earliest completion time

    Dim q : array   // tail

    Dim f : array   // earliest relative completion time

    Dim M : array

    // Calculation in table e

    $e_{0,j} = 0$, $\forall j = 1, ..., m$

    $e_{i,0} = 0$, $\forall i = 1, ..., n-1$

    $e_{i,j} = \max(e_{i,-1j}, e_{i,j-1}) + p_{\sigma_i,j}$, $\forall i = 1, ..., n-1, \forall j = 1, ..., m$

    // Calculation in table q

    $q_{n,j} = 0$, $\forall j = 1, ..., m$

    $q_{i,m+1} = 0$, $\forall i = 1, ..., n-1$

    $q_{i,j} = \max(q_{i,j+1}, q_{i+1,j}) + p_{\sigma_i,j}$, $\forall i = n-1, ..., 1, \forall j = m, ..., 1$

    // Calculation in table f

    $f_{i,0} = 0$, $\forall i = 1, ..., n$

    $f_{i,j} = \max(f_{i,j-1}, e_{i-1,j}) + p_{\sigma_n,j}$, $\forall i = 1, ..., n, \forall j = 1, ..., m$

    // Calculation in table M

    $M_i = \max_{j=1,...,m}(f_{i,j} + q_{i,j})$, $\forall i = 1, ..., n$

    Return M

End Function

Box 6.5. *Taillard algorithm: insertion of one piece*

Makespans M_i are then calculated by determining for every machine the delay which is caused by the insertion of the piece n in position i. Parts situated upstream before i are completed at the earliest possible time and those situated downstream are completed at the latest possible time, without impacting the makespan.

The functioning principle of the Taillard algorithm is shown in Figure 6.4. Using the data from the previous example, piece $\sigma_7 = 1$ is inserted in the partial solution $\overline{\sigma} = [5,7,4,2,3,6]$. Both the Gannt charts at the top correspond to the first two stages of the algorithm, namely, calculating the quantities $e_{i,j}$ and $q_{i,j}$. One can read for instance that $q_{4,1} = 55$ which means that at least 55 time units are necessary between the execution start of the 4th part (i.e. the part 2) and the end of the scheduling. On the chart at the bottom, piece one is inserted in the fourth position. Two blocks of parts are formed. Parts located before the position of insertion are placed on the left. Those located after are placed on the right. After placing operations of piece one at the earliest position (third stage: calculation of quantities $f_{4,j}$, $j = 1,...,m$), the makespan is obtained by making the block on the right slide until one of the operations that compose it comes to hit those already in place. This is represented by the black arrows on the diagram. Collision takes place on machine one, which determines the value of the makespan, 86 in this case.

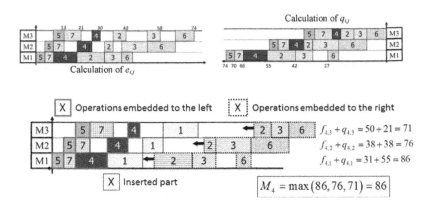

Figure 6.4. Taillard algorithm: insertion principle

Using the Taillard algorithm allows us to define efficient insertion neighborhoods. To generate a neighbor one must remove a piece among n

and apply this algorithm to determine the best position to re-insert it. As a result, the size of the neighborhood is reduced to n which allows us to explore it very quickly. The Taillard algorithm is very useful in metaheuristics, such as tabu search, that require in theory a full exploration of their neighborhood. Tabu search is the metaheuristic in which this technique was used for the first time. It is also very interesting for local search metaheuristics because it helps to find out faster if a solution is a local minimum.

6.3.2. *Variable-depth neighborhood search*

The use of large neighborhoods allows us to acquire local minima of better quality, but demands more calculation time. The effectiveness of methods based on local search consists of finding a compromise between these two contradictory tendencies. The works started by [LIN 73][1] and followed with the ejection chains, helped to provide response elements by bringing up the concept of variable-depth neighborhoods. Depth can be defined in an informal way as the "distance" which separates the current solution from its neighboring solutions. This distance is usually measured according to the characteristics that differentiate both solutions. The general idea is based on the notion that any global optimum is located at a certain distance from the current solution. By accepting in the neighborhood solutions that are distant enough, we are almost sure of finding an optimal solution there. The problem is that the exploration of this neighborhood, which grows in an exponential way, will not be accomplished at a reasonable time. The objective when using this type of neighborhood is trying to find out, guiding the exploration step by step, which are the characteristics to modify in order to go from any given solution towards an optimal solution.

6.3.2.1. *Effective suppression of a part*

The variable neighborhood search that we describe here is based on a succession of suppression-insertion of parts [DER 06]. Let us note first that the Taillard algorithm can easily be adapted to delete efficiently the part that one thinks is the least properly inserted in a permutation σ, as shown in Box 6.6.

The main difference between the insertion and the suppression algorithms is that the variable array f is no longer useful. By removing piece σ_i, the other parts are gathered in two blocks. Parts located upstream are embedded

---

1 These works are described in the chapter devoted to the traveling salesman problem (Chapter 5).

to the left (table e) and parts located downstream are embedded to the right (table q). By bringing the right block over the left block, one determines directly the makespan obtained by deleting σ_i.

The other differences are anecdotic and concern minor modifications regarding loops and indexes. These modifications are due to the fact that the suppression algorithm tries to remove a piece among n, while insertion adds a piece among $n-1$.

// Taillard's implementation – suppression of one piece
Function *Suppression_Taillard* $(\sigma : array, p : array, m : integer, n : integer)$

Dim e : array   // date of earliest completion time
Dim q : array   // tail
Dim M' : array
// Calculation of array e

$e_{0,j} = 0$, $\forall j = 1, \ldots, m$

$e_{i,0} = 0$, $\forall i = 1, \ldots, n$

$e_{i,j} = \max\left(e_{i,-1,j}, e_{i,j-1}\right) + p_{\sigma_i,j}$, $\forall i = 1, \ldots, n, \forall j = 1, \ldots, m$

// Calculation of array q

$q_{n+1,j} = 0$, $\forall j = 1, \ldots, m$

$q_{i,m+1} = 0$, $\forall i = 1, \ldots, n$

$q_{i,j} = \max\left(q_{i,j+1}, q_{i+1,j}\right) + p_{\sigma_i,j}$, $\forall i = n, \ldots, 1, \forall j = m, \ldots, 1$

// Calculation of array M'

$M'_i = \max_{j=1,\ldots,m}\left(e_{i-1,j} + q_{i+1,j}\right)$, $\forall i = 1, \ldots, n$

Return M
End Function

Box 6.6. *Taillard algorithm adapted: suppression of one part*

The principle of the suppression algorithm is shown in Figure 6.5. By deleting the fourth piece $\sigma_4 = 2$, parts 5–7–4 form the upstream block embedded to the left and parts 3–6–1 form the downstream block embedded to the right. The downstream block can move towards the left 13 time units before hitting the upstream block. The partial solution makespan $\overline{\sigma} = [5, 7, 4, 3, 6, 1]$ therefore amounts to 86–13=73. This delay defines the absolute gain g_i^{abs} obtained by deleting the ith piece (one has here $g_4^{abs} = 13$

time units). We also define the relative gain $g_i^{rel} = \dfrac{g_i^{abs}}{\sum_{j \in J} p_{\sigma_i, j}}$ as being the

absolute gain divided by the total processing time of the deleted piece. In this example, one has $g_4^{rel} = \dfrac{13}{23} \approx 56.5\%$.

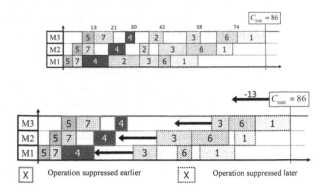

Figure 6.5. *Taillard algorithm adapted: principle for suppression*

By calculating the other values, one obtains g^{rel} = [30.8; 23.5; 50; 56.5; 57.7; 55.6; 38.7].. The most important relative gain is carried out with $\sigma_5 = 3$. This piece is considered to be the "least well-inserted" piece of all. The criterion of the relative gain seems more pertinent than the absolute gain. The most expensive parts are those which will generate *a priori* the most important absolute gains. The risk is, then, that by using the last criterion, those parts can, as a priority, be removed to the detriment of the cheapest parts to produce.

6.3.2.2. *Description of the neighborhood*

The algorithm shown in Box 6.7 is a variable-depth neighborhood in which a series of suppression and insertion operations is carried out. The position of the first piece to be deleted is provided in parameter. For any given permutation, it is, then, possible to create n neighboring permutations. Once this piece is deleted, it is re-inserted in the best position using the Taillard algorithm. At this stage, two situations are possible:

– either the obtained permutation (the movement completed corresponds to an insertion movement) is better than the current permutation. The

Boolean *found* takes the value TRUE and leads to exiting the loop. The result of the function is this new permutation;

– or the obtained permutation does not generate any improvement. The part which is considered the least properly inserted (as we defined above) is deleted and a new iteration is performed.

Two restrictions are added to this search: a tabu list (*TabuList*) and maximum search depth (*kmax*). The tabu list has all the parts that have been deleted since the start of the search. This is done to prevent the possibility of a cycle. The maximum search depth allows us to stop the search if for some reason no improvement is found in the course of the search. *kmax* is bounded above by the number of parts for two reasons. The first is technical and has to do with the management of the tabu list, which is restricted by the number of processed parts. The second one is of an intellectual type. The distance between any given permutation and an optimal permutation is at most n (if distance is defined by the minimal number of elements to be exchanged in order to pass from one permutation to the other).

The value of the Boolean *found* allows us to identify if an improvement is obtained during the descent. The value of k indicates the number of consecutive insertion movements which allowed us to achieve this improvement. We have called this movement k-insertion by analogy to movement k-opt of the TSP.

```
// Return position  pmin  from the smallest element of the array  t  whose part
σ (pmin)  is not in  S
Function  MinSearch(t : array, σ : array, n : integer, S : set) : integer
        Dim vmin, pmin : integer        // value and position of the minimum
        Dim i : integer                 // loop variable

        vmin = −∞
        pmin = 0
        For i =1 to n Do
                If ( t(i) < vmin  and  σ(i) ∉ S ) Then
                        vmin = t(i)
                        pmin = i
                End If
        End For
```

Return *pmin*

End Function

// Insert element *elt* at position *pos* in permutation σ

Procedure *insert_part* $(\sigma : array, elt : integer, pos : integer, n : integer)$

      Dim i : integer   // loop variable

      For i from n to pos **by -1 do**

$$\sigma(i+1) = \sigma(i)$$

      End For

$$\sigma(pos) = elt$$

End Procedure

// Delete and return the element located at position *pos* in the permutation σ

Function *delete_part* $(\sigma : array, integer, pos : integer, n : integer)$

      Dim i : integer   // loop variable

      Dim *elt* : integer

$$elt = \sigma(pos)$$

      For i from pos **to** n **Do**

$$\sigma(i) = \sigma(i+1)$$

      End For

      Return *elt*

End Function

Function
Mouvement_kl $(\sigma : array, p : array, posdep : integer, kmax : integer,$
$m : integer, n : integer) : integer$

      Dim σ' : array   // copy of permutation σ

      Dim *found* , *end* : boolean // stop flag

      Dim *job* : integer // current deleted part

      Dim H_x, H_y : integer   // cost of current and neighboring solution

      Dim *TabuList* : set   // set of tabu parts

      Dim M : array   // makespans obtained after Taillard's insertion or suppression

      Dim *pos* :integer   // stock successive insertion or suppression positions

      Dim k : integer   // current neighborhood depth

$\sigma' = \sigma$

$found$ = FALSE

end = FALSE

$k = 0$

$pos = posdep$

$H_x = makespan(\sigma', p, m, n)$

$job = delete\_part(\sigma', pos, n)$

$TabuList = \{job\}$

While *non trouve* et *non fin* **Do**

    $k = k + 1$

    $M = Insertion\_Taillard(\sigma', p, m, n)$

    $pos = MinSearch(M, n, \{pos\})$

    Call $insert\_job(\sigma', job, pos, n)$

    $H_y = makespan(\sigma', p, m, n)$

    If $H_y < H_x$ **Then**

        $found$ = TRUE

    Else

        If $k = kmax$ **Then**

            end = TRUE

        Else

            $M = Suppression\_Taillard(\sigma', p, m, n)$

            $pos = MinSearch(M, n, TabuList)$

            $job = supprime\_part(\sigma', pos, n)$

            $TabuList = TabuList \cup \{job\}$

        End If

    End If

End While

If *found* **Then**

    $\sigma = \sigma'$

End If

Return σ

End Function

Box 6.7. *Algorithm of the variable-depth neighborhood*

6.4. Results

Table 6.2 summarizes the results obtained with 10 Taillard instances made up of 50 parts and 20 machines. Those instances are especially difficult as they always resist the attacks of exact methods. We indicate in column "*LB-UB*" the best known lower and upper bounds of the optimal solution (updated: 22/05/2015 [Tai 15]). Here again, we find the construction heuristics "*CDS*" and "*NEH*", the local search with the neighborhoods exchange "*LS(E)*" and insertion "*LS(I)*" and iterated local search with the classic neighborhood insertion "*ILS (I)*" and the neighborhood k-I introduced in this chapter "*ILS (KI)*". Metaheuristics have run for 60 seconds. Results are given by estimating the relative gap to the best upper bound (i.e. the best known solution). Results provided for local searches are the average of 1,000 local minima, obtained from a random permutation generated with the Fisher–Yates shuffle. Those provided for the iterated local search are the average of 10 replications (10 executions by modifying only the germ of the random generator).

We must point out that construction heuristics provide relatively poor results even though NEH produces excellent results (up to 6.16 % of the best known solution). Local searches improve NEH but ultimately very little. With a classic iterated local search, one appreciably finds a 1% value. Results are practically divided by 2 with the neighborhood k-I.

	LB-UB	CDS	NEH	LS (E)	LS (I)	ILS (I)	ILS (KI)
TA051	3771- 3850	12,93	6,01	4,48	4,01	1,28	0,83
TA052	3668- 3704	14,18	6,21	5,02	4,57	0,80	0,38
TA053	3591- 3640	14,02	5,79	6,02	5,5	1,74	0,81
TA054	3635- 3723	12,61	6,03	5,02	4,48	1,08	0,68
TA055	3553- 3611	13,5	6,34	5,69	4,93	1,11	0,92
TA056	3667- 3681	11,99	5,97	4,67	4,23	1,11	0,77
TA057	3672- 3704	12,68	5,86	5,25	4,82	1,17	0,76
TA058	3627- 3691	12,29	6,25	5,99	5,46	1,50	0,87
TA059	3645- 3743	14,11	6,02	4,75	4,29	1,28	0,92
TA060	3696- 3756	15,04	6,55	5,61	5,16	0,95	0,70
Average		13,34	6,10	5,25	4,75	1,20	0,76

Table 6.2. *Results for the problem of the permutation flow shop*

6.5. Conclusion

This chapter has allowed us to show how the ideas introduced for the traveling salesman problem could be successfully reinvested for the permutation flow-shop.

Results seem less impressive that those of TSP but they are very good. By giving more time to the iterated local search (60 minute replications), these movements have allowed us to find two new upper bounds for the famous Taillard instances. We show a detailed account of those solutions below:

TA054 – New upper bound 3720 (against 3723).

SOLUTION.– 5 11 14 21 30 13 38 24 12 7 45 35 20 31 48 37 32 50 19 33 43 3 44 49 39 29 46 10 17 9 42 22 6 26 47 40 15 36 4 27 2 25 18 8 23 41 34 1 16 28.

TA055 – New upper bound 3610 (against 3611).

SOLUTION.– 40 48 4 2 19 31 50 28 20 49 34 5 23 21 32 25 43 45 44 18 26 36 33 42 27 16 41 14 8 47 39 38 10 6 22 17 30 12 13 3 37 9 7 1 46 24 15 29 35 11.

Some Elements for
Other Logistic Problems

So far, we have worked with so-called permutation problems; that is to say, problems that can be naturally represented in the form of a permutation σ. The two problems that we have used as case studies are the traveling salesman problem and the permutation flow-shop problem.

In Chapter 4, we learned base techniques that allow implementing metaheuristics for permutation problems in a general way. Chapters 5 and 6 helped to describe advanced techniques that improve the performance of these methods.

We are going to see now how this knowledge can be enlarged to deal with other problems: that is to say, combinatorial optimization problems that do not belong to the permutation problem class.

We shall begin with an introductory section having two approaches that will be applied in many cases. Other sections will deal with applications for particular logistic problems.

7.1. Direct representation versus indirect representation

For many combined optimization problems, permutation does not constitute a natural representation of a solution. There are then two possibilities:

– either one works on a direct representation of the solution;

– or, it is possible to create a complete solution of the problem thanks to the permutation. We can say then that permutation is an indirect representation of this solution.

Let us come back one instant to the direct presentation, which is probably the most classical and natural approach. Metaheuristics work directly on the solution space. Their implementation needs to develop the components required for a proper functioning; for instance, the elaboration of a neighboring system, crossover or mutation operators, etc. It is an additional effort in terms of the conception of metaheuristics. Nevertheless, this effort gives us the opportunity to integrate knowledge elements of the problem in metaheuristics.

In the case of the indirect representation, it would suffice to conceive a function $F : S \to \Omega$ which associates to every permutation $\sigma \in S$ a solution $x \in \Omega$ of our problem. It is then completely possible to implement a metaheuristic that works on the total number of permutations. The advantage of such a procedure is that the application of metaheuristics is simply accomplished by reutilizing the elements seen on Chapter 5. The most important setback of this approach is related to the respective size of search spaces S and Ω.

If $|S| \ll |\Omega|$ then some solutions of the problem are unattainable. This case is shown in Figure 7.1. Space S of permutations is projected through function F in a subset $F(S) \subset \Omega$. If there is an optimal solution $x^* \notin F(S)$, this one is unattainable. The best solution that can be provided by a metaheuristic based on this type of indirect representation will be the solution y^* that verifies $H(y^*) = \underset{x \in F(S)}{opt}\ H(x)$. One clearly has $H(y^*) \geq H(x^*)$. In certain cases, equality can be established. It makes sense, when one applies this kind of procedure, to raise the question of accessibility for an optimal solution and try to demonstrate this equality.

The case where $|S| \gg |\Omega|$ is less usual. This implies that space Ω is smaller than the permutation space; solutions, then, are probably easy to manipulate by a direct representation. In that case, many permutations lead to the same solution. Let us take the example of an eight-object knapsack. From a permutation σ_1, one goes through objects in the order indicated to determine which ones are stored inside the knapsack. Let us suppose that we place objects 1, 3, 4, 5 and 7 and that we reject objects 2, 6 and 8. Permutations $\sigma_2 = [1,3,4,5,7,2,6,8]$, $\sigma_3 = [7,5,4,3,1,8,6,2]$ and many others will lead to the same solution. Classical neighborhood systems for permutations can be adapted to guarantee that two neighboring permutations will lead to two different solutions.

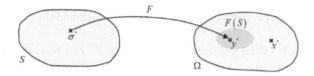

Figure 7.1. *Indirect representation: case of an unattainable global optimum*

7.2. Conditioning problems

Listed below are some elements that will give us a good start with the conception of metaheuristics for the knapsack and bin-packing problems.

7.2.1. *The knapsack problem*

Many works deal with the multidimensional knapsack that is an extension of the classical problem. Let K be a set of dimensions. The knapsack holds a capacity C_k on each dimension $k \in K$ (mass, volume, prices, etc.). Furthermore, every object $i \in I$ has its own characteristics for each dimension $m_{i,k}$. The multidimensional problem leads to verify the capacity constraint on every dimension of the problem.

In the linear problem (Box 2.5), this would replace constraint [2.10] by constraints:

$$\sum_{i \in I} m_{i,k} \times x_i \leq C_k, \forall k \in K \tag{2.10a}$$

We will continue discussing the resolution procedures for the classic knapsack problem. Taking into account the multidimensional aspect does not generate a special integration problem.

As discussed in the above section, we used the example of the knapsack solved by indirect representation. This procedure is possible but seems of little interest compared to a direct representation. The latter will be the focus of our concerns.

A knapsack solution is naturally represented by binary vector x_i corresponding to the variables of the linear programming. For every solution, set I can be split into two subsets $I^+ = \{i \in I \,/\, x_i = 1\}$ and $I^- = \{i \in I \,/\, x_i = 0\}$, which contain, respectively, objects stored in the sack and the others.

A solution is called saturated if no object $i \in I^-$ can be stored in the sack without violating the capacity constraint. It is clear that every optimal solution is saturated (assuming that $v_i > 0, \forall i \in I$). Metaheuristics will focus its search on the subspace of saturated solutions, where one is certain that an optimal solution can be found.

The classic neighborhood systems for the knapsack problem are:

– removing and filling: this movement consists of removing k objects from the sack and replacing them with I^- objects until saturation;

– storing and removing: this movement consists of adding k objects to the sack and removing I^+ objects if the capacity of the sack is exceeded;

– variable-depth search: An ejection chain can be used by applying a succession of "removing and filling" movements with $k = 1$. The tabu list can be defined by forbidding, for instance, to remove any object that has been added to the sack since the movement started.

7.2.2. The bin-packing problem

7.2.2.1. Indirect representation

In the one-dimension bin-packing problem, let us remember that the goal is to store a set of objects in a minimum number of bins (assumed to be identical).

This problem can be solved with an indirect representation. Given a permutation σ that determines an order over the objects, a solution can be determined by applying one or another of the heuristics "*next fit*", "*first fit*" or "*best fit*".

– the "*next fit*" principle is the following. The first bin is designated as the current bin. Objects are gone over in sequence and are placed in the bin. When this is no longer possible, the current bin is closed and the object is placed in the next bin that becomes the current bin;

– in "*first fit*", all the bins are assumed to be open from the start. One goes over the objects in sequence and places them in the first bin that can hold them;

– finally, the heuristic "*best fit*" places objects in the bin that can hold them and which is the most full.

It can be easily proven that every optimal solution can be found.

7.2.2.2. *Direct representation*

In the case of a direct representation, binary variables $x_{i,j}$ of the linear program (Box 2.5) with $1 \le i, j \le n$ can be reused (it is important to remember that, in the worst-case scenario, the number of bins is equal to the number of objects). In a similar way, we can use a vector x' of integers, for which $x'_i = j$ means that object i is in the bin $j (x_{i,j} = 1)$.

A specific issue of this problem must be overcome to apply neighborhood methods that can be at least slightly effective. The reason for this problem lies in the minimizing criterion, which is the number of bins required for the whole set of items. This criterion is not discriminating enough and too many solutions will have the same value. The purpose is to find a more discriminating criterion that would allow us to separate two solutions that have the same number of bins, by giving preference to that one which is the closest to "emptying" a bin. [FLE 02] proposed to maximize the sum of square of the masses in each bin. This objective function is expressed as:

$$Max\ f(X) = \sum_{j=1}^{n} \left(\sum_{i=1}^{n} m_i^2 x_{ij} \right)$$

and this is how a problem of minimization can become a problem of maximization! The role of this objective function is shown in the Figure 7.2. We can see that the best possible solution is certainly X_1, which is the one with the "most empty" bins, and therefore is the closest to a solution that includes only two bins.

Classic neighborhoods can be defined as the displacement of an item from one bin to another (as long as the destination bin has enough capacity to hold it), or the exchange of two items stored in two different bins (likewise, as long as it is made possible by the capacity of bins).

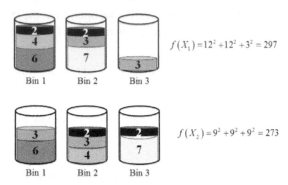

$$f(X_1) = 12^2 + 12^2 + 3^2 = 297$$

$$f(X_2) = 9^2 + 9^2 + 9^2 = 273$$

Figure 7.2. *Bin packing problem – example of objective function*

7.3. Lot-sizing problems

We show how metaheuristics can be applied for the capacitated lot-sizing problem (CLSP). This part relies on the work thesis of [LEM 08], who proposed some metaheuristics for this problem.

Let us remember that the problem lies in determining for each period $t \in T$ of the horizon whose products are to be manufactured among a set I and in which quantity in order to respond to a demand $d_{i,t}$, the purpose being to minimize the sum of inventory and production costs.

The CLSP linear program (Box 2.10) uses binary variable $Y_{i,t}$ that indicates the products whose production is started at each period, and the integer variable $X_{i,t}$ that specify the manufactured quantities. The variable $Y_{i,t}$ that are easily deducted from variables $X_{i,t}$ ($X_{i,t} > 0 \Leftrightarrow Y_{i,t} = 1$) allow to define an indirect representation; while variable $X_{i,t}$ is a direct representation of the solution.

Using variable $Y_{i,t}$ we must know how to find the quantities to be produced $X_{i,t}$. That can be accomplished by solving the linear program in which variable $Y_{i,t}$ is fixed, or with heuristics. Both techniques have their pros and cons. The first technique is expensive in terms of calculation time while the second one does not guarantee that the optimal solution will be found.

[LEM 08] proposes several neighborhood systems for direct representation. First, he points out that a solution is only attainable when the stock levels of products (variables $S_{i,t}$ in the linear program) stay in positive numbers for every period. He concludes that using a simple neighborhood scheme, that would consist in choosing a product and displacing a quantity from one period to another, would have very little chance to succeed.

The author then lists a certain number of characteristics that determine the quantities to be displaced; this allows him to define several neighborhood guiding techniques, and to improve the effectiveness of metaheuristics.

7.4. Localization problems

In this metaheuristic application for localization problems, we shall consider the problem of dynamic localization. The objective is to determine, on each period $t \in T$, which are the warehouses $i \in I$ that will be open. Variable $y_{i,t}$ of the mathematical program (Box 2.12) allows us to define a direct representation of a solution. Every client is assigned to the warehouse which is the closest to him. In cases where warehouses have a capacity and the clients a demand to be satisfied, the optimal allocation of clients is obtained in a polynomial time by solving a transport problem (section 3.2.2). By knowing $y_{i,t}$, it is possible to estimate the total cost that corresponds to the represented solution.

A solution is, therefore, perfectly represented by a binary matrix. The neighborhoods could be defined by modifying one value of the matrix (which corresponds to the opening and closing of a site). The only concern is taking into account the constraint that only authorizes a single change of state on the horizon. Let us take as an example a problem with six periods and let us assume that a warehouse $i \in I$ opens in period three. In the representation of this solution, the third column will be then $'y_i = (0,0,1,1,1,1)$. The neighbor obtained by modifying the value at the period $t = 5$ will be represented by $'y_i = (0,0,1,1,0,1)$ and does not correspond to a feasible solution. By taking a closer look at this example, one notices that the only periods for which a change of state is authorized are periods 2 and 3; this corresponds to representations $'y_i = (0,1,1,1,1,1)$ and $'y_i = (0,0,0,1,1,1)$. This means that the warehouse opens at period 2 or at period 4. One has, therefore, advanced or retarded the change of state by one period.

This gives a notion for an effective neighborhood, and which consists of:

– choosing a warehouse randomly;

– determining the two possible periods for a change of state;

– choosing one of the two periods and apply the change of state at random.

```
// Determine the period to apply the change of state for the warehouse i₀
// NT is the number of periods of the horizon
Function CalculPeriod (Y : array, i₀ : integer, NT : integer)
            dim choice : integer          // choice of first or second neighbor
            dim t₀ : integer              // period

         choice ← alea(0,1)
         // case of a warehouse open or closed on the horizon
         Si Y(i₀,1) = Y(i₀,NT) Then
                    If choix = 0 Then
                            t₀ ← 1
                    Else
                            t₀ ← 0
                    End If
            Else
                    // case of a warehouse that opens or closes over the horizon
                    t₀ ← 2
                    While Y(i₀,1) = Y(i₀,t₀) Do
                            t₀ ← t₀ + 1
                    End While
                    If choice = 0 Then
                            t₀ ← t₀ - 1
                    End if
            End if
            Return t₀
End Function
```

Box 7.1. *Pseudo algorithm for the construction of the neighborhood*

The case of a warehouse that closes during the studied horizon is similar to the previous case. It must be clarified what happens when the warehouse does not change of state on the horizon. When it is closed over the horizon, we have $'y_i = (0,0,0,0,0,0)$ and the two possible neighborhoods will be by $'y_i = (1,0,0,0,0,0)$ and $'y_i = (0,0,0,0,0,1)$. When it is open on the horizon, $'y_i = (1,1,1,1,1,1)$. The neighbors will be represented by $'y_i = (0,1,1,1,1,1)$ and $'y_i = (1,1,1,1,1,0)$. For both cases, the changes of state take place in the first or the last period of the horizon.

The function shown in 0 determines randomly, for a warehouse i_0 given in parameter, one of the two possible periods. Once we have defined i_0 and t_0, the instruction $Y(i_0, t_0) \leftarrow 1 - Y(i_0, t_0)$ allows to construct the neighbor solution (this instruction turns 0 into 1 and 1 into 0). The same instruction allows going back to the current solution.

7.5. Conclusion

We showed in this chapter, without dwelling on the details, how metaheuristics could be applied on combinatorial optimization problems that are not the permutation type. We could see two types of approaches: direct representation and indirect representation, each having its pros and cons. Difficulty is inherent in the problem; whichever choice is made to represent a solution will be found somewhere.

The last part of this book is devoted to the application of metaheuristics for the supply chain management. All the logistic problems, considered up to now separately, will be tackled together in order to integrate in the optimization process some interactions between the actors and the activities that can be encountered in a supply chain.

PART 3

Evolutions and Current Trends

Supply Chain Management

So far, we have studied logistic problems separately. We were able to show the difficulties of each, mostly due to their algorithmic complexity, and stress the importance of metaheuristics to solve them. Throughout this chapter, dedicated to supply chain management, we will find that all these problems are related, linked by a "horizontal synchronization", with an effort of coordination by the different actors and/or the different activities present in the supply chain, and linked also by a vertical synchronization, so that decisions taken at any given level (strategic, tactical or operational) are consistent with decisions taken at other levels.

8.1. Introduction to supply chain management

[GAN 95] defines the supply chain as follows: "A supply chain is a network of facilities and distribution options that performs the functions of procurement of materials, transformation of these materials into intermediate and finished products, and the distribution of these finished products to customers". Figure 8.1 shows a classic supply chain with the actors that intervene and different flow types that go through it (physical, information or financial).

To the activities of purchasing, production and distribution that appear in this definition, we can also add activities for stocking finished products, as well as raw materials and semi-finished products.

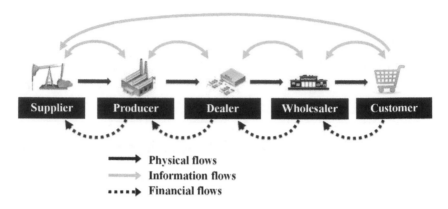

| Supplier | Producer | Dealer | Wholesaler | Customer |

——▶ **Physical flows**
⇒ **Information flows**
••••▶ **Financial flows**

Figure 8.1. *General sketch of a supply chain*

All these activities, shown in Figure 8.2, as well as the actors, from rank 2 suppliers to final customers, must collaborate for the proper functioning of the supply chain. Needless to say, the vision that we give is simplified. Each partner is not necessarily involved in the whole range of activities. It is not difficult to find companies that subcontract their stocking and/or their distribution activities to focus on their "core business" activity, which is production.

Supply chain management was first mentioned by [OLI 82] and has developed progressively since the 1960s to devise an efficient supply chain. [SIM 03] describes supply chain management as "a set of methods used to effectively coordinate suppliers, producers, depots, and stores, so that commodity is produced and distributed at the correct quantities, to the correct locations, and at the correct time, in order to reduce system costs while satisfying service level requirements".

8.2. Horizontal synchronization of the supply chain

To stress the importance, for all the actors in the supply chain, of coordinating their decisions, we will first introduce the beer game. We will then draw conclusions in terms of management.

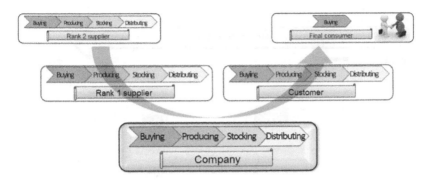

Figure 8.2. *Supply chain: a vision by activities*

8.2.1. *The beer game*

The beer game is a business game created in the MIT (Massachusetts Institute of Technology) in the 60s by J.W. Forrester, following his work on system dynamics [FOR 61]. This game is widely used both in the industrial and the university world. The purpose is to coordinate a beer supply chain with four players (factory, distributor, wholesaler and retailer). Each player takes the role of one of these actors and has control over his own beer stock. He must decide at every game turn (for instance, one day) the amount of beers that he should request to his direct supplier in order to meet the demand of the customer who only the retailer knows. He is inclined to request a small amount since every article in stock has a cost, but in a quantity that is enough to prevent running out of stock, which also generates a cost. The restraint imposed to players is that they must not communicate with each other about the amounts ordered. Another important feature of the game lies in the delivery times, which are very important and must be taken into account. An order placed on Monday is processed on Wednesday (two days later) and is received on Friday (two more days). The goal is trying to minimize the sum of all costs (inventory and backorder) on the whole retail chain.

Figure 8.3 shows the game board of a beer game conducted by students as part of their supervised project, directed to a group of high-school students and renamed for the occasion "the milk carton game". The actors are the farm, the dairy, the distribution platform and the shopping center. The top of the board is reserved to the order placement, that is to say, to the information flow. The lower part processes physical flows through product stock management.

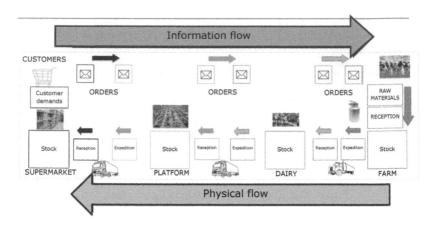

Figure 8.3. *Gameboard of the milk carton game*

The beer game participants, with very limited exceptions, always reach the same conclusion. One notices an oscillating and amplifying phenomenon. Before elaborating further on these phenomena, we are going to disclose the secret of the game. The customer's demand is equal to four packing units during the first four periods of the game, then, it remains steady with eight units for the rest of the game. For my part, the only information that I pass to the players at the beginning of the game is that an important advertising campaign has been launched by the brand, and that a significant increase in sales is expected during the next few days.

The swinging phenomenon comes due to the fact that the drop in the level of supply leads players to increase their orders, causing stock-outs which in turn leads again to a an increase in the orders, sometimes to senseless levels. Once delivery times have been met, big amounts go to stock, easily covering previous stock-outs. Players do not place orders during several game turns. Thus, players alternate between periods of serious stock-outs and periods of overstocking.

This is an amplifying phenomenon where the more one distances oneself from the retailer and, therefore, from the customer's demands, the more significant the amplitude of swing will be.

This phenomenon is known as the bullwhip effect, also called the Forrester effect. The next section is dedicated to the answers which can be used to counter this effect.

8.2.2. *The bullwhip effect*

The bullwhip effect is a phenomenon that affects a supply chain when fluctuations over orders are more important than those over demands. This translates into a demand for swinging that become bigger and bigger as one goes up the supply chain (Figure 8.4).

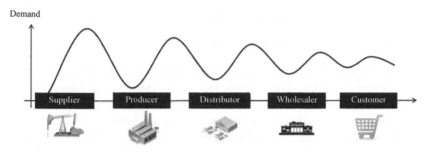

Figure 8.4. *The bullwhip effect in a supply chain*

According to [MIR 06], the bullwhip effect results mainly from four causes:

– processing of the customer demand: faulty information can spread along the supply chain if the ordering policies depend on local rules. This phenomenon can be amplified if delivery times are long. This usually happens in the beer game;

– batch ordering policies: these policies are used legitimately in companies because of economic reasons (transport optimization, purchases of big quantities). However, they generate variations in demand that can favor the bullwhip effect;

– price fluctuations: during promotional operations, the actors of the supply chain have a tendency to increase their stocks to meet an increase of demand, and to reduce their orders over the following periods. As previously, this generates variations in the demand;

– rationing and shortage of products: when demand is superior to production capacity, suppliers give priority to the biggest orders. As a result, certain customers can have a tendency to inflate their orders, to be well-stocked as soon as possible, and then consume the surplus.

[WIK 91] propose five strategies to limit the consequences of the bullwhip effect, which they study in a three-level supply chain:

– improve the rules of decision on every echelon;

– refine the definition of parameters for the existing rules of decision;

– reduce delivery times;

– reduce the length of the distribution chain;

– improve the information quality all along the supply chain.

The implementation of these solutions needs the full participation of all those members of the supply chain. [KOU 06] defines coordination as any action or approach which leads the actors of a logistical system to act in order to improve the functioning of the system as a whole. In a decentralized organization, in which every actor is independent, every single decision must, therefore, be made in favor of common interest rather than in one's own interest.

It is all these collaborating aspects, intended to improve the total functioning of the supply chain, that we collect under the term horizontal synchronization.

8.3. Vertical synchronization of a supply chain

[SCH 00] introduces models of logistical networks taking into account the three decision-making levels: strategic, tactical and operational (Figure 8.5).

The strategic level is concerned with long term considerations (in general more than 18 months) and collects all decisions that have an impact on the conception of logistical network. The latter must be able to evolve in time, so it can be a useful accompaniment for geostrategic choices defined by the leaders of the firm. Localization problems make it possible to provide an answer for this kind of conflicts.

The tactical level gathers decisions taken over a mid-term horizon (1 to 18 months). These decisions will have an effect on the sizing of the logistical network. The objective will be to determine all of the means required (production, distribution or human resources), and which will permit to meet a projected demand while trying to minimize costs. We shall find at this level the tactical planning problems that are part of lot-sizing issues.

The operational level is concerned with all decisions over a short-term horizon (less than one month). The objective will be to pilot the logistical chain by trying to respect delivery times. This level gathers problems of production scheduling, conditioning or transport.

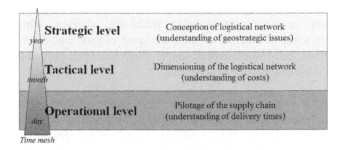

Figure 8.5. *The three decision-making levels*

Each level interacts with the others. Does the logistical network conceived at the strategic level allow to respond to demand forecasts? Also, is the planning of production capacity accomplishable at operational level? [LEM 08] defines the concept of vertical synchronization, which consists of organizing all the decisions over time to guarantee coherence and feasibility among levels.

8.4. An integral approach of the supply chain

Adopting a unified version of the supply chain is to consider the system as a whole, integrating all the activities (buying, producing, stocking and distributing), all the actors (suppliers, producers, wholesalers, retailers, consumers) and all the decision-making levels (strategic, tactical and operational). According to [DER 14] this integration is functional, temporal and geographical:

– functional integration affects mainly the synchronization of physical flows. It is born from the need to synchronize the flows of raw materials and semi-finished products to meet the customer demands. The Materials Requirement Planning (MRP) [ORL 75] method partially responds to this need;

– temporal integration lies on the Manufacturing Resource Planning (MRP II) method [WRI 84], which is an evolution of MRP (by taking into account capacities of supply, production, stocking, and financial distribution).

MRP II leans on breaking down of the temporal horizon in five plans: the strategic plan, the industrial and business plan (IBP), the master production plan (MPP), the net requirements calculation (NRC) and shop floor control;

– geographical integration incorporates the multi-site dimension. The MRP II approach is originally defined for the mono-site companies. Current organizations are increasingly using multi-site schemes, which involve decisions in terms of location of sites, transport of products, consideration of delivery times, etc. The concept of supply chain management can be seen as a general version of the MRP II approach.

Figure 8.6 shows issues to be solved by actors of the supply chain for every activity and for each decision-making level. All the logistical problems that have been used as an example are found in this figure. Localization problems deal with the conception of logistical networks (which include networks of supplies and networks of distribution) at the strategic level. Lot-sizing problems are production planning issues at the tactical level. The problems of scheduling and transport are found at the operational level for the activities involved. Packing problems are the exception since, even though they correspond to the operational level, they do not correspond to one of the mentioned activities. These problems occur at the level of the order preparation and vehicle loading and are part of stocking and distribution activities. They are also one of the actors in the supply chain: the person in charge of stock and the carrier.

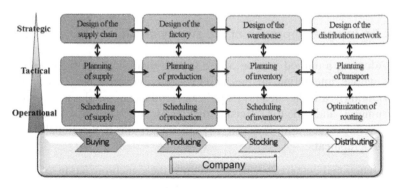

Figure 8.6. *Optimization problems of a supply chain*

We have seen that several logistical problems, which coincide with some cases of the figure, are NP-class problems and are subject to an algorithm complexity. The current trend is taking interest on what happens at the arrow levels; that is, to construct problems that cover two adjacent squares. [GRI 12] note the interest of these issues that they call hybrid (we will reserve the term hybrid to describe the methods) and also the use of metaheuristics to solve them.

Metaheuristics has the advantage of allowing two types of problem-solving approaches, the integrated approach and the hierarchical approach:

– an integrated problem-solving approach involves treating a problem as a whole. The main difficulty is in conceiving a full representation of the solution and of the neighborhood systems able to work on this representation. The disadvantage of this approach is that very often it has problems to guide effectively metaheuristics towards a high quality solution;

– a hierarchical approach involves breaking a problem down in various subproblems and applying an optimization method (metaheuristic or exact method) on each sub problem. This natural procedure leads to conceiving a hybrid method. A drawback is that by working more or less separately on both problems, the hybrid method will be more controlled but could miss the global optimum.

8.5. Conclusion

We were able to highlight the benefits of considering the supply chain as a whole. Thus, we have defined the notion of horizontal synchronization which is used in the collaboration of the different actors that are part of the supply chain, and in the coordination of flows among different activities. We also defined vertical synchronization as a method to take coherent decisions at different levels.

We have also seen the rise of new concerns that result in an interface of classical logistical problems and which are more difficult to solve than their elders. Hybrid metaheuristics have all the qualities that we need to cope with those problems. We will devote the next chapter to these matters.

9

Hybridization and Coupling Using Metaheuristics

In this last chapter dedicated to metaheuristics, we will describe two advanced techniques called metaheuristics-based hybridization and coupling. We shall begin by pointing out the benefits that these techniques can bring for dealing with problems of optimization related to supply chain management, before going into the details.

9.1. Metaheuristics for the optimization of the supply chain

In order to optimize the functioning of the supply chain, it is necessary to overcome many difficulties:

– *Model the supply chain*: the diverse entities (actors, activities, products, sites) that take part in the supply chain must be defined, as well as their interactions. The development of the knowledge-based model is often a consuming and cumbersome task.

– *Overcome algorithm complexity*: theoretical problems, like those we have worked with so far, are not polynomials and, therefore, difficult to solve. We must take into account two factors that make real problems even more difficult than academic problems. On the one hand, real problems often lead to instances where big size issues must be solved. On the other hand, real problems integrate management rules or specific constraints that must be taken into account.

– *Overcome structural complexity*: ask an industrialist to specify the criteria that enables him to judge if his system is efficient. Performance criteria of a supply chain are most often based on the minimization of expenses and the maximization of customer service rate–criteria that can be difficult to assess, and are contradictory at the same time. However, the postulate that enables us to set up an optimization method must be able to compare solutions from a quantitative point of view.

– *Know how to retrieve all relevant data*: in companies, a huge amount of data floats around. These data are often present under various forms, in the various information systems of the firm, in tools like the spreadsheets, in data bases prepared in-house and in files or paper documents. Still it is necessary to know where to retrieve data that one could need, and how to arrange them so they can be processed.

– *Manage uncertainties*: certain data are perfectly known, others are based on predictions, sometimes with important uncertainties. In a general fashion, the more distant the considered horizon is, the more strategic their decisions to be taken become, and the more they are based on uncertain data.

[LOU 01] underlines the paramount role that metaheuristics can play as decision aid tools for the supply chain. These methods actually have the qualities to solve the difficult optimization problems that can play a role in the supply chain management. Reasons cited are as follows:

– metaheuristics are usually simple, easy to implement, robust and have proven to be useful to solve many difficult optimization problems;

– their modular nature leads to short development and maintenance times, important qualities for the purpose of industrial integration;

– their capacity to manipulate huge masses of data, which allows us to integrate the whole complexity of the problem in the solution procedure rather than having to aggregate data or simplify the problem and work on a problem that only partially represents reality;

– their capacity to manage uncertainties, being able to study several scenarios instead of proposing an exact solution based on a model in which most data are estimated.

The hybridization of methods will give answers that are likely to counter the algorithmic complicacy of problems addressed, while coupling will help us to cope with structural complexity, uncertainties and other hazards.

9.2. Hybridization of optimization methods

[BLU 11] point out that more and more optimization methods do not strictly follow the paradigm of a single method but combine algorithmic components that can come from several optimization fields. That is how they define hybrid methods. In addition, the authors propose a state-of-the-art view of the hybridization techniques used in the literature, with metaheuristic and other techniques of operational research (constraint programming, tree search, dynamic programming, etc.).

The interest of hybridization is to exploit the advantages of each method used. Of course, we will talk about hybridization based on metaheuristics if one of the method components comes from a metaheuristic.

9.2.1. Classification of hybrid methods

[TAL 02] proposes a taxonomy of hybrid methods that is shown in Figure 9.1. The author proposes a hierarchical classification in accordance to two criteria: the nesting level and the cooperation level. If this classification is originally proposed for the hybridization of metaheuristics, it can easily be extended to the case where one (or even both) of the hybridization methods do not correspond to a metaheuristic. Within the context of the metaheuristic-based hybridization, at least one method is a metaheuristic. We shall make use of the term method (understood as optimization method) instead of metaheuristic:

– the nesting level defines how methods are inter-connected. In a low-level hybridization, one of the methods is used as a component of another. Conversely, in a high-level hybridization, methods are independent of each other, in the sense that none of them intervenes in the internal functioning of one another;

– the cooperation level defines how all methods work together. In a sequential hybridization, methods are used one after the other; a method's output is used as the input for the next method. In a cooperative hybridization, methods act as agents that roam the search space independently and then cooperate by pooling together the fruits of their research.

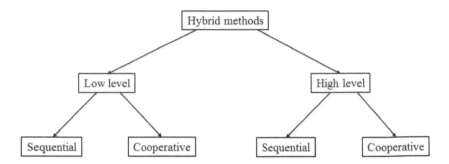

Figure 9.1. *Taxonomy of hybrid metaheuristics (according to [TAL 02])*

Four classes of hybrid methods are thus defined. Each of them is illustrated through the following examples.

9.2.2. Illustration by example

– *Low-level sequential class*: in this class of hybrid methods, one finds the "individual-based metaheuristics/local search" hybridizations that are detailed in the next section. Local search is used as a component of the metaheuristic. (Every new solution generated by the metaheuristic is locally optimized). The metaheuristic and the local search work in a sequential way. The metaheuristic provides a solution for local search which sends back a local minimum.

– *Low-level cooperative class*: this class has hybridizations of the type "population-based metaheuristics/local search". During iteration, the metaheuristic generates several individuals, all of which are locally optimized. At that moment, the metaheuristic regains control of operations and decides what to do with local minima obtained.

– *High-level sequential class*: every form of hybridization in which a method is used after the other belongs to this category. A trivial case of greedy method functions as initialization to metaheuristics.

– *High-level cooperative class*: the last method class is undoubtedly the least intuitive. We can use the example of the algorithm "Tribes" [COO 08] that is a variation of particle swarm optimization. The objective of tribes is to conceive an auto-adaptive metaheuristic that sets its own parameters. The swarm is divided in tribes, each one containing one or several particles; the best representative is called the shaman. Tribes work as independent swarms, which share information through the shamans from time to time. After these exchanges, Tribes evolve through time (migration from particles from one tribe to an other, death or birth of particles).

9.2.3. "Metaheuristic/local search" hybridization

"Metaheuristic/local search" hybridization is certainly the most widespread form of hybridization. The idea is to combine the exploring power of metaheuristics (especially population-based metaheuristics) with the great capacity of search methods to exploit the search space.

The general principle of the "metaheuristic/local search" hybridization is shown in Figure 9.2. Every metaheuristic has within it a component that allows us to generate new solutions. The idea of this hybridization is to apply a local search from each of its solutions. The latter sends back to the metaheuristic the local minimum obtained. The metaheuristic follows its process with this local minimum instead of the solution that was initially generated. In absolute terms, this kind of hybrid method amounts to applying the general scheme of the metaheuristic to the space of local minimum rather than to the entire search space. The results obtained are usually far better than when using the metaheuristic alone.

This hybrid method, therefore, has the double benefit of being efficient and easy to implement. This explains its success in the 1990s. Thus, the hybridization "simulated annealing/local search" has been used by [MAR 92, MAR 96] and [DES 96]. The hybridization of genetic algorithms with local search was started by [MOS 89]. It gave rise to a class of evolutionary algorithm called *Memetic Algorithms*. A bit later, [FRI 96] used the term *Genetic Local Search* to define the same category of hybrid methods. Hybridization between ant colony algorithm and local search was used by [STÜ 97] for the traveling salesman problem. Finally, [DER 05] proposed a framework for the hybridization "particle swarm optimization/local search" also applied to the traveling salesman problem.

9.2.4. Metaheuristic hybridization/Exact Methods

Hybridization between a metaheuristic and an exact method is an especially interesting technique. It combines the advantages of exact methods and those of metaheuristics, which are particularly complementary.

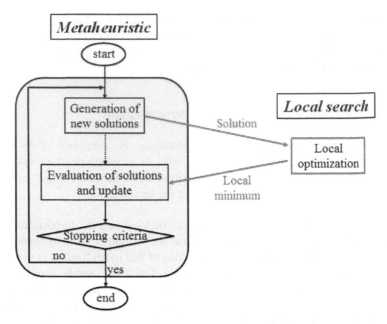

Figure 9.2. *Principle of the hybridization "metaheuristic/local search"*

The advantages of exact methods are:

– if resolution is possible, finding an optimal solution (with proof of optimality);

– otherwise providing lower and upper bounds to the optimal solution;

– fragmenting the search space where an optimal solution is situated.

The advantages of metaheuristics are:

– performing well in big-size instances;

– evaluating great number of solutions in short periods;

– being able to easily integrate new variables of a problem and being flexible;

– being based on a simple principle and easy to implement.

[DIM 03] proposed a state of the art in which he lists five major categories of "metaheuristics/exact method" hybridization:

– *Large neighborhood search*: being able to explore large-sized neighborhoods by guiding the search with an exact method. For instance, the neighborhood "hyper-opt" for the traveling salesman. This neighborhood uses the concept of "hyperedge". A hyperedge of size k is defined by a succession of k consecutives edges. The hyperopt neighborhood consists of choosing two hyperedges of size k that do not overlap, deleting all the edges that they contain while reconstructing a new solution. The number of possibilities increases exponentially with k; an exact method can be used to find the best neighbor.

– *Exploitation of the good solution structure*: this kind of approach works in two phases. The first phase consists of obtaining a set of good solutions. The second phase involves exploiting this pool of solutions to build a sub-problem that can be solved by an exact method. It is used, for instance, by [BIX 99]. The authors explain that by proceeding this way, they were able to find an optimal solution for the instance "fl1577", from a sample with 25 solutions acquired with a Lin & Kernighan-type heuristic in which no optimal solution appeared. This instance comes from the TSPLIB and contains 1,577 cities. The subproblem involves looking for a traveling salesman solution in a graph where the 1,577 cities are the vertices, whose edges are only present in one of the 25 solutions of the sample.

– *Using lower bounds in greedy heuristics*: greedy heuristic based on a local optimum choice which allows building a solution step-by-step. The idea is to make a choice with a criterion that relies on the search for lower bound.

– *Directing the search to promising space zones*: these techniques are based on relaxations of the linear problem that can be solved in an optimal way. These optimal solutions are then used to precise the search space in which the metaheuristic will evolve.

– *Improving the metaheuristic*: to use an exact method as a component of a metaheuristic, for instance, in the perturbation of an iterated local search.

As proof of the interest generated by the "metaheuristic/exact method" hybridization, a number of authors have published reviews on this kind of approach [PUC 05, JOU 09].

9.3. Coupling of optimization methods and performance evaluations

We shall talk of method coupling to indicate that, like hybridization, we are going to combine two methods. The difference is that the latter are of a different nature. First, we are going to clarify these concepts before introducing some optimization/simulation couplings applied to the supply chain management.

9.3.1. *Double complexity*

A supply chain is, by its own nature, a complex system, made up of many entities that interact according to specific rules in different decision-making levels. Furthermore, the objective pursued by every actor of the chain is often summarized as optimizing costs and guaranteeing a certain service quality. Therefore, evaluating the performance of a supply chain is not something that is easy to define.

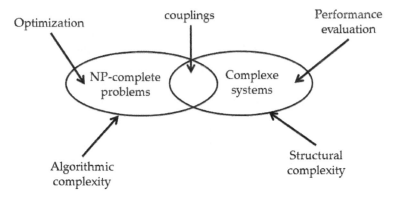

Figure 9.3. *Double complexity and method coupling [NOR 05]*

[NOR 05] introduced the concept of double complexity to characterize these systems. An algorithmic complexity which represents the inherent difficulty linked to the resolution of the underlying combinatorial optimization problems and a structural and functional complexity, which represents the difficulty of evaluating the performance of the system.

The author promotes using a coupling with an optimization method (metaheuristic or other) and a performance-evaluation method (model of deterministic or stochastic simulation, Markovian models, etc.) to take into account this double complexity (Figure 9.3).

9.3.2. *Coupling of optimization method/simulation model*

We propose for this part to emphasize two different approaches for optimization-simulation coupling applied to supply chain management.

[ABO 11] points out that the benefit of the optimization-simulation coupling in the context of the supply chain management lies on several points. According to the authors, determining the choice that would optimize the performance criterion of a supply chain is tricky:

– to acquire a mathematical description of the function to be optimized is not possible because of correlations, often complex, that link the actors of the supply chain together and that have an influence on its performance;

– supply chains are often characterized by several objectives, sometimes contradictory, that need to make choices, sometimes arbitrary, among several alternatives or scenarios. The huge number of decision variables and possible scenarios make any comprehensive listing or simulation impossible. This point agrees with the concept of double algorithmic and functional complexity as mentioned before;

– optimization methods must take into account the uncertainties present in a supply chain to devise robust solutions.

This vision implies that the simulation model is restricted to the performance evaluation of one solution proposed by the optimization method. This is a master-slave type of coupling, in which simulation acts as a black box that corresponds to a low-level hybridization. This approach is shown in Figure 9.4.

[ALM 09] also proposes an optimization-simulation coupling, but with an iterative sequential approach, similar to a high-level hybridization. The authors propose two action models of the same supply chain: a detailed model to which a discrete event simulation method is applied and an aggregate linear model which is solved with a linear solver. The supply chain considered has three levels (suppliers, producers and clients). The goal is to meet the clients' demand while minimizing costs (production, penalties for delay, etc.). The proposed approach is the following (Figure 9.5): the result of several simulations helps to define the aggregated values (averages) that work as an input to the linear model. The latter solves the aggregated model. Decision variables obtained this way are reinjected into the simulation model and the process is repeated as many times as required.

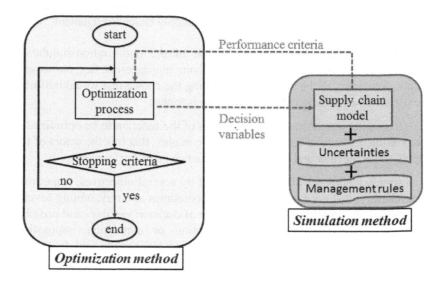

Figure 9.4. *Optimization-simulation coupling (1st approach)*

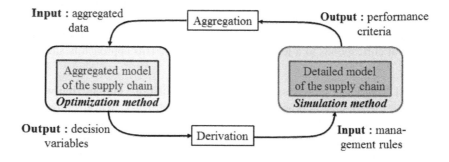

Figure 9.5. *Optimization-simulation coupling (2nd approach)*

9.4. Conclusion

We had the opportunity to describe some solution approaches that integrate metaheuristics, and which help to cope with the algorithmic and functional complexities of the logistics systems. These approaches, based on hybridization and coupling, have a significant potential. The purpose of the next two chapters is to demonstrate this. In Chapter 10, we shall study a workshop problem that combines the transport and production activities (horizontal synchronization), and conception and scheduling problems (vertical synchronization). In Chapter 11, we will introduce two problems built around the vehicle routing problem: the inventory routing problem (horizontal synchronization) and the location routing problem (vertical synchronization).

10

Flexible Manufacturing Systems

This chapter discusses the Flexible Manufacturing Systems (FMS); many studies have been dedicated to this matter in the french laboratory (Laboratory of Computer Science, Modelisation and Optimization) (LIMOS)) at Clermont-Ferrand. This problem is only a link of the supply chain that corresponds to the production activity. It is true that the FMS are logistic systems that make it possible to cope with all vertical synchronization problems, from conception to steering flows, including dimensioning.

We would like to show in this chapter that taking into account the lower decision-making level can generate better decisions at the higher level.

10.1. Introduction to the FMS challenges

FMS are totally automated systems, gathering productions means (machines or flexible cells) that are interconnected by a transportation network. The transportation is accomplished, for instance, by an electric guidance system, optical fiber (wire guidance) or rail tracks which allow autonomous vehicles to move around the workshop. The downside of these systems is that they require a heavy investment, but they can reduce long-term cost because of their flexibility and adaptability.

Figure 10.1 shows four classic FMS layouts with four machines, which are those used in the case library that will serve as test. The LU (Load/Unload) station is the place of entry and exit of the parts for the system. The arrows indicate the path sense on each section of the transportation network. We can notice that certain sections are uni-directional or bi-directional.

The FMS have been studied over the last couple of decades with a wide range of problems, which can be distributed in three major categories: workshop design, transportation network design and scheduling problems:

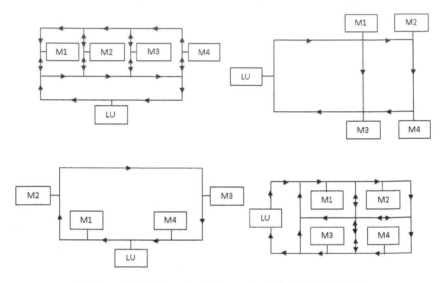

Figure 10.1. *Four classic layouts of the FMS [BIL 95]*

– the workshop design is often modeled with the *"Facility Layout Problem"*. This problem must not be confused with the *"Facility Location Problem"* (a site location problem that we had already seen in section 2.7). The goal is to determine how machines, occupying a certain surface on the floor, must be arranged in such a way that the estimated flows of products that will circulate in the workshop be kept at a minimum. [DRI 07] offer a state-of-the-art solution for this problem. These issues lie in the strategic-decision level;

– the following problem deals with the design of the transportation network and encompasses several subproblems. The first is the design of the guiding system itself. The choice of uni-directional or bi-directional sections is important. Bi-directional sections help to reduce travel times but makes traffic management more vulnerable. The second problem is precisely traffic management when it is necessary to anticipate collision problems between vehicles. The third subproblem is localization of the pick-up and drop-off areas on the machines (these zones are in the interface between the production system and the transport system). The last point concerns vehicles themselves. How many should we have, what characteristics to choose in terms of transport capacity – in terms of speed, etc.?

– finally, the steering issues of the FMS are scheduling problems that are separated in two categories: off-line and on-line problems. The off-line problems are placed at a high operational level. Traffic problems are disregarded. The role of these problems is to make a predictive scheduling. Travel times for going from one machine to the other are perfectly determined. In the on-line problems, the scheduling is reactive. The traffic is now taken into account and the trajectory of vehicles is determined as a function of the state of the system when it starts a displacement. For example, the transport network can be fragmented into elementary sections. A vehicle cannot be authorized to penetrate a new section if there is already another vehicle inside the section. This helps to avoid any collision risk.

Vis [VIS 06] and Le-Anh and De Koster [LEA 06] provide interesting views to discover design and steering issues of transport networks.

10.2. The job-shop problem with transport

As a first step, the simultaneous scheduling of machines and material handling system is presented. This problem was first defined by Ülusoy and Bilge [ULU 93, BIL 95, ULU 97]. This problem has been studied by many authors. Here, we present our contribution to this problem [DER 08]. However, the description that we present of the simulation model is much more detailed that that of the referenced article.

10.2.1. *Definition of the problem*

The problem at hand is an off-line scheduling problem. The workshop is deemed to be the job-shop type. A set of parts must undergo operations in a certain sequence. Every operation is performed on a determined machine on a determined span. As illustrated in Figure 10.2 the 10 sets of parts (designated as jobset 1–10) will serve for the tests. For example, part no. 1 of jobset no. 1 must undergo three operations. The first on machine M_1 during 8 t.u., the second on M_2 during 16 t.u. and the third on M_4 during 12 t.u. For all the parts, we include a last operation that takes place on the LU station and that has a zero operating time. The goal of this fictitious operation is to force the parts to leave the system once their manufacturing is over.

Jobset 1: (5 parts)
$p_1 : M_1(8), M_2(16), M_4(12)$
$p_2 : M_1(20), M_3(10), M_2(18)$
$p_3 : M_3(12), M_4(8), M_1(15)$
$p_4 : M_4(14), M_2(12)$
$p_5 : M_3(10), M_1(15)$

Jobset 2: (6 parts)
$p_1 : M_1(10), M_4(18)$
$p_2 : M_2(10), M_4(18)$
$p_3 : M_1(10), M_3(20)$
$p_4 : M_2(10), M_3(15), M_4(12)$
$p_5 : M_1(10), M_2(15), M_4(12)$
$p_6 : M_1(10), M_2(15), M_3(12)$

Jobset 3: (6 parts)
$p_1 : M_1(16), M_3(15)$
$p_2 : M_2(18), M_4(15)$
$p_3 : M_1(20), M_2(10)$
$p_4 : M_3(15), M_4(10)$
$p_5 : M_1(8), M_2(10), M_3(15), M_4(17)$
$p_6 : M_2(10), M_3(15), M_4(8), M_1(15)$

Jobset 4: (5 parts)
$p_1 : M_4(11), M_1(10), M_2(7)$
$p_2 : M_3(12), M_2(10), M_4(8)$
$p_3 : M_2(7), M_3(10), M_1(9), M_3(8)$
$p_4 : M_2(7), M_4(8), M_1(12), M_2(6)$
$p_5 : M_1(9), M_2(7), M_4(8)$

Jobset 5: (5 parts)
$p_1 : M_1(6), M_2(12), M_4(9)$
$p_2 : M_1(18), M_3(6), M_2(15)$
$p_3 : M_3(9), M_4(3), M_1(12)$
$p_4 : M_4(6), M_2(15)$
$p_5 : M_3(3), M_1(9)$

Jobset 6: (6 parts)
$p_1 : M_1(9), M_2(11), M_4(7)$
$p_2 : M_1(19), M_2(20), M_4(13)$
$p_3 : M_2(14), M_3(20), M_4(9)$
$p_4 : M_2(14), M_3(20), M_4(9)$
$p_5 : M_1(11), M_3(16), M_4(8)$
$p_6 : M_1(10), M_3(12), M_4(10)$

Jobset 7: (8 parts)
$p_1 : M_1(6), M_4(6)$
$p_2 : M_2(11), M_4(9)$
$p_3 : M_2(9), M_4(7)$
$p_4 : M_3(16), M_4(7)$
$p_5 : M_1(9), M_3(18)$
$p_6 : M_2(13), M_3(19), M_4(6)$
$p_7 : M_1(10), M_2(9), M_3(13)$
$p_8 : M_1(11), M_2(9), M_4(8)$

Jobset 8: (6 parts)
$p_1 : M_2(12), M_3(21), M_4(11)$
$p_2 : M_2(12), M_3(21), M_4(11)$
$p_3 : M_2(12), M_3(21), M_4(11)$
$p_4 : M_2(12), M_3(21), M_4(11)$
$p_5 : M_1(10), M_2(14), M_3(18), M_4(9)$
$p_6 : M_1(10), M_2(14), M_3(18), M_4(9)$

Jobset 9: (5 parts)
$p_1 : M_3(9), M_1(12), M_2(9), M_4(6)$
$p_2 : M_3(16), M_2(11), M_4(9)$
$p_3 : M_1(21), M_2(18), M_4(7)$
$p_4 : M_2(20), M_3(22), M_4(11)$
$p_5 : M_3(14), M_1(16), M_2(13), M_4(9)$

Jobset 10: (6 parts)
$p_1 : M_1(11), M_3(19), M_2(16), M_4(13)$
$p_2 : M_2(21), M_3(16), M_4(14)$
$p_3 : M_3(8), M_2(10), M_1(14), M_4(9)$
$p_4 : M_2(13), M_3(20), M_4(10)$
$p_5 : M_1(9), M_3(16), M_4(18)$
$p_6 : M_2(19), M_1(21), M_3(11), M_4(15)$

Figure 10.2. *The 10 data sets [BIL 95]*

In a more formal framework, a J set of parts must be manufactured on a M set of machines. Each part $p_j \in J$ must undergo n_j operations. Let $n = \sum_{p_j \in J} n_j$ be the total number of operations to schedule.

$I = \{op_1, \ldots, op_n\}$ represents the whole set of operations. This set is fragmented in as many subsets as there are parts; we will notice I_j the subset associated to part p_j. Operations are numbered according to the following convention: $I_j = \{op_{N_j+1}, \ldots, op_{N_j+n_j}\}$ with $N_j = \begin{cases} 0 \text{ if } j=1 \\ \sum_{l=1}^{j-1} n_l \text{ if } j > 1 \end{cases}$.

For example, for job set 1, we have $I_1 = \{op_1, op_2, op_3, op_4\}$, $I_2 = \{op_5, op_6, op_7, op_8\}$, etc. Among these operations, we differentiate the routing initial operations whose set is denoted by $\underline{I} = \{op_i \,/\, \exists p_j \in J, i = N_j + 1\}$ ($op_1 \in \underline{I}$ and $op_5 \in \underline{I}$) and the routing final operations $\overline{I} = \{op_i \,/\, \exists p_j \in J, i = N_j + n_j\}$ ($op_4 \in \overline{I}$ and $op_8 \in \overline{I}$). All the rest are routing mid-range operations.

To every production operation, we can associate a noted transport operation $\tilde{I} = \{\widetilde{op_1}, \ldots, \widetilde{op_n}\}$. We will designate, respectively, MO_i, MD_i and d_i the origin machine, the destination machine and the processing time associated to operations op_i and $\widetilde{op_i}$. For the range-starting operations ($op_i \in \underline{I}$) we put down $MO_i = LU$ and for the range-ending operations ($op_i \in \overline{I}$) we put down $MD_i = LU$ and $d_i = 0$. Through our example, $MO_1 = LU$, $MD_1 = M_1$ and $d_1 = 8$; $MO_2 = M_1$, $MD_2 = M_2$ and $d_2 = 16$; etc.

Defining the origin machine and the destination machine for each operation will simplify the rest of our description, and specially the discrete-event simulation engine.

In what follows, we will often use op_i to designate interchangeably the production or transport operation associated $\widetilde{op_i}$.

Let K be the set of vehicles (all assumed to be identical). Concerning the movement of vehicles between the various machines, we will designate, respectively, $TC(M_i, M_j)$ and $TV(M_i, M_j)$ loaded travel time and unloaded travel time conditions for every couple of machines $(M_i, M_j) \in M^2$. The loaded travel times can encompass, in addition to the distance covered, the load and unload time of the parts. In the examples discussed in the literature, times under load and with no load are identical. The matrices, calculated from the configuration Figure 10.1 are shown in Figure 10.3.

Layout 1	LU	M1	M2	M3	M4
LU	0	6	8	10	12
M1	12	0	6	8	10
M2	10	6	0	6	8
M3	8	8	6	0	6
M4	6	10	8	6	0

Layout 2	LU	M1	M2	M3	M4
LU	0	4	6	8	6
M1	6	0	2	4	2
M2	8	12	0	2	4
M3	6	10	12	0	2
M4	4	8	10	12	0

Layout 3	LU	M1	M2	M3	M4
LU	0	2	4	10	12
M1	12	0	2	8	10
M2	10	12	0	6	8
M3	4	6	8	0	2
M4	2	4	6	12	0

Layout 4	LU	M1	M2	M3	M4
LU	0	4	8	10	14
M1	18	0	4	6	10
M2	20	14	0	8	6
M3	12	8	6	0	6
M4	14	14	12	6	0

Figure 10.3. *Problem of policy*

10.3. Proposal for a metaheuristic/simulation coupling

To solve this problem, we proposed a solution approach based on a metaheuristic/simulation coupling. We present at first how a solution is represented, and then we describe our discrete-event simulation engine before going to the description of the metaheuristic and to the presentation of some results.

10.3.1. *Representation of a solution*

Most papers in the literature propose a representation based on the job-shop approach. Travels are taken into account through a management rule of the type "first available vehicle". The representation that we proposed takes the opposite view. It is based on the vehicle routing problem. It is then that the production times are determined through a management rule. We effectively assume that vehicles discharge products at the upstream stock of machines, the latter being run by a *first in, first out* (FIFO) policy. There is no policy for the downstream stock of machines. Vehicles load the parts for which they have been programmed, regardless of the running order on the machine.

The solution is represented by the list of transport operations that each vehicle is to carry out. An example is shown in Figure 10.4, always based on jobset one. Eighteen transport operations must be carried out. The partition of operations by part is called back. The first vehicle starts moving part no. 2 from loading station LU on machine M_1 (operation op_5), then returns to load part no. 5 on LU station to place it finally on machine M_3 (operation op_{16}), etc.

Partitioning of operations by part

$$I_1 = \{op_1, \ldots, op_4\} \quad I_2 = \{op_5, \ldots, op_8\} \quad I_3 = \{op_9, \ldots, op_{12}\}$$
$$I_4 = \{op_{13}, op_{14}, op_{15}\} \quad I_5 = \{op_{16}, op_{17}, op_{18}\}$$

List of transport operations assigned to each vehicle

Véhicule 1	op_5	op_{16}	op_{14}	op_9	op_2	op_{11}	op_3	op_8		
Véhicule 2	op_{13}	op_1	op_6	op_{10}	op_7	op_{17}	op_{15}	op_{12}	op_4	op_{18}

Figure 10.4. *Partitioning of operations and representation of one solution*

10.3.2. Simulation method

The simulation model that has been developed follows an event-driven approach. When an event is performed, the clock of the simulator advances to the corresponding instant and updates the system, having the ability to create or modify other events.

The principle of simulation is based on the concept of feasible operation. For an operation op_i to be feasible, the two following conditions must be respected:

– *operation can go into production*: this a range start operation $(op_i \in I)$ or the previous operation op_{i-1} has been performed;

– *the associated transport operation can be performed*: op_i is situated in the first position on a vehicle or the previous operation has been performed.

Let us start the simulation by focusing on jobset one with workshop configuration 1 and the representation shown in Figure 10.4. At $t = 0$, the only operations that can go into production are those of range start. They are grouped in the set $NP = I$ ($NP = \{op_1, op_5, op_9, op_{13}, op_{16}\}$ in our example). The operations that can be conveyed correspond to the first tasks assigned to vehicles. If these operations can be placed in the set NT, we have $NT = \{op_5, op_{13}\}$.

The set of operations that can be performed at $t = 0$ is obtained with the intersection $NP \cap NT$. In this case, we have $NP \cap NT = \{op_5, op_{13}\}$. An event is generated for each feasible operation. This requires determining the date on which the vehicle will unload the part on the destination machine. In our example, vehicle one transports part no. 2 onto machine M_1 at the date $TC(LU, M_1) = 6$ and vehicle two finishes the transport of part no. 4 at the date $TC(LU, M_4) = 12$.

Among the events created, the first one in chronological order is chosen; it corresponds to a certain operation op_i (op_5 on the example). The simulation advances to the corresponding date ($t = 6$). The resources used (namely, vehicle one and machine M_1) are requisitioned to carry out their transport and production task. They will again be available on the date six for the case of the vehicle, and on the date $6 + 20 = 26$ for the case of the machine (for the record $d_5 = 20$).

Sets NP and NT are then updated in turn. As the operation op_i is completed, it is removed from both sets. The operation that follows it in its operating range op_{i+1} becomes available and is added in NP unless if $op_i \in \bar{I}$ (range-ending operation). Likewise, in regard to transport, the next operation programmed on the vehicle becomes available and is added in NT, unless $\widetilde{op_i}$ was the last position on the vehicle. In our case, we shall have $NP = \{op_1, op_6, op_9, op_{13}, op_{16}\}$ and $NT = \{op_{16}, op_{13}\}$. A new event is created for every supplementary operation in $NP \cap NT$ (at most two events will be generated for every event that has occurred). In our example, operation op_{16} generates a new event at the date $6 + TV(M_1, LU) + TC$ $(LU, M_3) = 6 + 6 + 10 = 22$, time that is needed to let the vehicle go find part no. 5 at the loading station (the part is supposed to be available at the workshop entry) then take it to machine M_3.

Simulation continues taking place. The detailed algorithm is shown in Box 10.1. The following notations are used in addition to those previously introduced:

– $ind(k)$: index that points to the vehicle's current transportation k;

– $busy(m)$: date until which machine M_m is busy;

$- t_K(i), t_M(i), \forall op_i \in I$:   respectively   the   completion   time   of transportation $\widetilde{op_i}$ and of operation op_i on machine MD_i ;

$- nt(k)$: number of transports programmed for vehicle k ;

$- \sigma(k,i), k \in \{1,...,|K|\}, i \in \{1,...,nb(k)\}$ (represents   the   evaluated solution): the ith transport carried out by vehicle k .

Additionally, the simulation uses a procedure $create\_event(k,i,t)$ that creates an event at date t for vehicle k and operation $\widetilde{op_i}$ and a function $next\_event(\ )$ that retrieves information related with the next event (vehicle, operation, time) in a chronological order.

At the end of the simulation model execution, two cases are possible. Either all operations have been scheduled, or some of them could not. In the first case, the solution is feasible and it is possible to calculate several performance criteria, including the makespan which is the one that draws our interest in this study. In the second case, we have a deadlock situation (none of the operations available for transport is for production; the solution is not feasible. As a result, the simulation engine allows us to determine the feasibility of one solution.

For $k = 1,...,|K|$ **Do** $ind(k) = 1$ **End For**

For $m = 1,...,|M|$ **Do** $busy(m) = 0$ **End For**

For $i = 1,...,|I|$ **Do** $t_K(i) = +\infty$ **End For**

For $k = 1,...,|K|$ **Do**

    $op_i = \sigma\big[k, ind(k)\big]$

    If $op_i \in \underline{I}$ **Then**

            $create\_event\big(k, i, TC[MO_i, MD_i]\big)$

    End If

End For

While there are events **Do**   (Main loop)

    $(k,i,t) \leftarrow next\_event(\ )$

    $t_K(i) = t$

    If $op_i \in \overline{I}$ **Then**

        $t_M(i) = t_K(i)$

Else
$$t_M(i) = \max\left[busy\left[(MD_i)\right], t_K(i)\right] + d_i$$
$$busy[MD_i] = t_M(i)$$

End If

// Creation of an event related to transport

If $ind(k) < nb(k)$ **Then**
$$ind(k) = ind(k) + 1$$
$$op_{i'} = \sigma\left[k, ind(k)\right]$$

If $op_{i'} \in I$ **Then**
$$create\_event\left(k, i', t + TV[MD_i, MO_{i'}] + TC[MO_{i'}, MD_{i'}]\right)$$

Else If $t_T(op_{i'-1}) < +\infty$ **Then**
$$create\_event\left(k, i', T_1 + TC[MO_{i'}, MD_{i'}]\right)$$
$$\text{where } T_1 = \max\left[t + TV[MD_i, MO_{i'}], t_M(i'-1)\right]$$

End If

End If

// Creation of an event related to the routing

If $\left(op_i \notin \overline{I}\right) \wedge \left(\exists k' \in \{1, \ldots, |K|\}, k' \neq k \, / \, \sigma\left[k', ind(k')\right] = op_{i+1}\right)$ **Then**

If $ind(k') = 1$ **Then**
$$create\_event\left(k', i+1, T_2 + TC[MD_i, MD_{i+1}]\right)$$
$$\text{where } T_2 = \max\left(TV[LU, MD_i], t_M(i)\right)$$

Else
$$op_{i_{prec}} = \sigma\left[k', ind(k') - 1\right] \quad \text{// previous operation on the vehicle}$$
$$create\_event\left(k', i+1, T_3 + TC[MD_i, MD_{i+1}]\right)$$
$$\text{where } T_3 = \max\left(t_T(i_{prec}) + TV\left[MD_{i_{prec}}, MO_{i+1}\right], t_M(i)\right)$$

End If

End If

End If

End While

Box 10.1. *Problem of policy*

10.3.3. *Optimization method*

The optimization method used is an iterated local search (section 3.3.4). The components of this metaheuristics are the following:

– local search is a stochastic descent based on two movements, which are the exchange of two operations and the insertion of one operation. These movements are guided so as to take into account the precedence constraints related to routing of parts. The purpose is restricting movements to the operations that take place in tight-time windows. The rule used is the same for both movements. A first operation op_i is picked at random. One determines an interval that corresponds to the dates of completion time for previous and next operation in the routing of the part. The second operation is now chosen among those whose completion time date is included in this interval. To be more specific, if $op_i \in \underline{I}$ (range start), the considered interval is $\left[0; t_M(i+1) \right]$, if $op_i \in \overline{I}$ (end of range) the interval is $\left[t_m(i-1); +\infty \right]$ otherwise, the interval is $\left[t_M(i-1); t_M(i+1) \right]$. As soon as both operations are determined, the type of movement (exchange or insertion) is chosen at random with a 0.5 probability for each movement;

– the perturbation involves applying three times the previous neighborhood, making sure that the generated solution remains feasible;

– the acceptance criterion is the simulated annealing type with a temperature that follows a geometrical law. The temperatures used are the following: the starting temperature is $T_0 = 5$; the stoppage temperature is $T_a = 10^{-3}$ and the rate is calculated so that 1,000 descents are carried out in every instance.

10.3.4. Results

We present results obtained with the classic instances used in the literature. These do not take into account the fictitious operations for the return of parts to the LU station. The combination of 10 job sets with the four configurations allows constructing 40 instances. The instance "$Exa\beta$" is constructed from job set α and from layout β. For each of these instances, two vehicles are used. Both vehicles and the set of parts are located at the LU station at date 0.

Results are shown in Table 10.1. Three methods are compared: "B&U" represents the best result reported in the three articles [ULU 93, BIL 95, ULU 97], column "GAA" gives the results obtained with a genetic algorithm by [ABD 04] and column "SALS" shows the results that we have obtained with the approach introduced here. For every method, we show the makespan obtained and the relative gap with respect to the best known solution in the year 2008 (best result presented in the above-mentioned articles). The average for the 40 instances is also shown in the last line of this table.

A negative result then, shows that we have improved the best known solution; that is the case for 11 of the 40 instances. For the rest, we find the best solution of the literature. Calculation time was in the region of a few seconds for the $6 + TV(M_1, LU) + TC$ biggest instances on a standard PC in the year 2008.

In spite of several works published after this study ([RED 06], [CHA 11] and [LAC 13]), results have not been improved significantly. The reason probably lies in the fact that literature instances are small-sized (about 20 operations) and are not selective enough to differentiate the most recent methods. Proof of this is the considerable robustness of SALS, which practically finds the best known solution on each of its replications. This behavior with metaheuristics helps us to surmise that the results provided are very close to the optimal.

Inst.	B&U		GAA		SALS	
Ex11	96	0.00	96	0.00	96	0.00
Ex12	82	0.00	82	0.00	82	0.00
Ex13	84	0.00	84	0.00	84	0.00
Ex14	103	0.00	103	0.00	103	0.00
Ex21	104	1.96	102	0.00	100*	-1.96
Ex22	76	0.00	76	0.00	76	0.00
Ex23	86	0.00	86	0.00	86	0.00
Ex24	113	4.63	108	0.00	108	0.00
Ex31	105	6.06	99	0.00	99	0.00
Ex32	85	0.00	85	0.00	85	0.00
Ex33	86	0.00	86	0.00	86	0.00
Ex34	113	1.80	111	0.00	111	0.00
Ex41	116	3.57	112	0.00	112	0.00
Ex42	88	0.00	88	0.00	87*	-1.14
Ex43	91	2.25	89	0.00	89	0.00
Ex44	126	0.00	126	0.00	121*	-3.97
Ex51	87	0.00	87	0.00	87	0.00
Ex52	69	0.00	69	0.00	69	0.00
Ex53	75	1.35	74	0.00	74	0.00
Ex54	97	1.04	96	0.00	96	0.00

Inst.	B&U		GAA		SALS	
Ex61	121	2.54	118	0.00	118	0.00
Ex62	98	0.00	98	0.00	98	0.00
Ex63	104	0.00	104	0.00	103*	-0.96
Ex64	123	2.50	120	0.00	120	0.00
Ex71	118	2.61	115	0.00	111*	-3.48
Ex72	85	7.59	79	0.00	79	0.00
Ex73	88	2.33	86	0.00	83*	-3.49
Ex74	128	0.79	127	0.00	126*	-0.79
Ex81	161	0.00	161	0.00	161	0.00
Ex82	151	0.00	151	0.00	151	0.00
Ex83	153	0.00	153	0.00	153	0.00
Ex84	163	0.00	163	0.00	163	0.00
Ex91	117	0.00	118	0.85	116*	-0.85
Ex92	102	0.00	104	1.96	102	0.00
Ex93	105	0.00	106	0.95	105	0.00
Ex94	123	0.82	122	0.00	120*	-1.64
Ex101	150	2.04	147	0.00	147	0.00
Ex102	137	0.74	136	0.00	135*	-0.74
Ex103	143	1.42	141	0.00	138*	-2.13
Ex104	164	3.14	159	0.00	159	0.00
Average		1.23%		0.09%		-0.53%

Table 10.1. *Comparative results with the instances of the literature [DER 08]*

10.4. Workshop layout problem

10.4.1. *Aggregated model and exact resolution*

We come to the actual objective of this section. We consider that the FMS under study is already configured, both at production cells and at guiding network level. We also assume that it is possible to reorganize the workshop by simply reordering the production zones, without modifying its structure. This modification could be made at a tactical level, to allow SFP adapting to a market evolution or to the launching of new products that entail a modification of flows in the system.

This issue is shown in Figure 10.5. On the left the original configuration as defined in the job shop instances with transport and on the right the skeleton of this configuration where production areas are presented (numbered from L1 to L5). We will use the term L for this set. The purpose is therefore to determine the allocation of machines for production zones in order to minimize the flows of products. This issue is modeled as a quadratic allocation problem [KOO 57] (Box 10.2). Constraints [10.2] and [10.3] are similar to those of the allocation problem. Every machine is allocated to a single location and reciprocally each location hosts one and only one machine. The objective function [10.1] minimizes the sum of traveling times for the whole set of products. It should be stressed that this not a linear program. The objective function is quadratic.

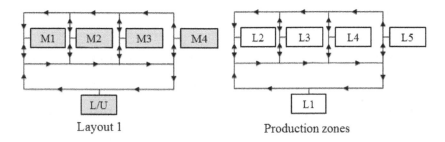

Layout 1   Production zones

Figure 10.5. *Reorganization of the workshop*

The results obtained by solving this problem are summarized in Table 10.2. The locations are defined according to the original configurations as follows: zone L1 corresponds to the L/U station and zones L2 to L5 correspond to machines M1 to M4 respectively. For the instance "Ex11", the optimal allocation involves placing machine M2 in location L1, machine M4 in location L2, etc. This machine allocation is the one that minimizes the sum of traveling times for products in the workshop.

Data:

$I = \{op_1, \ldots, op_n\}$: all operations

$t_{l,l'}, \forall (l, l') \in \{1, \ldots, |M|\}$: traveling times between zones l and l'

$MD_i, MO_i, \forall op_i \in I$: origin machine and destination machine of operation op_i

Variables:

$$x_{ml} = \begin{cases} 1 \text{ if machine } M_m \text{ is in the zone } L_l \\ 0 \text{ otherwise} \end{cases}, \forall (m, l) \in \{1, \ldots, |M|\}$$

Minimize:

$$\sum_{op_i \in I} \sum_{l \in \{1, \ldots, |M|\}} \sum_{l' \in \{1, \ldots, |M|\}} t_{l,l'} \times x_{MO_i, l} \times x_{MD_i, l'} \qquad [10.1]$$

Under the constraints

$$\sum_{m \in \{1, \ldots, |M|\}} x_{m,l} = 1, \forall l \in \{1, \ldots, |M|\} \qquad [10.2]$$

$$\sum_{l \in \{1, \ldots, |M|\}} x_{m,l} = 1, \forall m \in \{1, \ldots, |M|\} \qquad [10.3]$$

Box 10.2. *Mathematical formalization of the quadratic assignment problem*

Instances	QAP Assign	Cost	Instances	QAP Assign	Cost
Ex11	(2,4,LU,1,3)	182	Ex61	(LU,1,2,3,4)	156
Ex12	(1,3,4,2,LU)	114	Ex62	(LU,1,2,3,4)	60
Ex13	(4,LU,1,3,2)	140	Ex63	(LU,1,2,3,4)	84
Ex14	(3,2,4,1,LU)	214	Ex64	(2,3,4,1,LU)	168
Ex21	(LU,1,2,3,4)	144	Ex71	(2,3,4,LU,1)	186
Ex22	(1,2,3,4,LU)	60	Ex72	(LU,1,2,3,4)	84
Ex23	(LU,1,2,3,4)	84	Ex73	(LU,1,2,3,4)	112
Ex24	(3,4,LU,2,1)	156	Ex74	(3,4,LU,2,1)	204
Ex31	(4,LU,1,2,3)	152	Ex81	(LU,1,2,3,4)	164
Ex32	(1,2,3,4,LU)	66	Ex82	(LU,1,2,3,4)	60
Ex33	(LU,1,2,3,4)	98	Ex83	(LU,1,2,3,4)	84
Ex34	(1,2,3,LU,4)	166	Ex84	(1,2,3,LU,4)	160
Ex41	(1,3,2,LU,4)	172	Ex91	(1,2,4,LU,3)	146
Ex42	(3,LU,4,1,2)	96	Ex92	(4,LU,3,1,2)	60
Ex43	(LU,1,2,3,4)	140	Ex93	(1,2,4,LU,3)	84
Ex44	(4,1,3,2,LU)	200	Ex94	(1,2,4,3,LU)	148
Ex51	(3,4,2,1,LU)	130	Ex101	(LU,1,2,3,4)	184
Ex52	(3,4,1,2,LU)	74	Ex102	(LU,2,1,3,4)	84
Ex53	(4,1,2,LU,3)	98	Ex103	(2,1,3,4,LU)	112
Ex54	(3,2,4,LU,1)	152	Ex104	(1,3,4,2,LU)	190

Table 10.2. *Comparative results in the literature instances [DER 13]*

Based on this table, the decision maker can determine the foreseeable location for machinery. The solution provided guarantees that product flows, which coincide with the travels that the vehicles are responsible for, are minimal for the corresponding configuration. On the other hand, the model does not integrate in its evaluation the unloaded travel times of vehicles. We will subsequently designate this solution with the term QAP-optimal solution.

The second part of the study allows precisely for taking into account the travels of vehicles. To do this, the evaluation model will be fine-tuned. We are going down one level and use our previous works on simultaneous scheduling of production and transport resources. The optimization methods developed in section 10.3 will help to evaluate more precisely the machine assignment provided by the solution provider, and to find out if other assignments are preferable.

10.4.2. Detailed model and approximate solutions

The proposed solution approach relies on the aggregated model presented in the previous section. This one provided the QAP-optimal solution. There is no doubt that this solution has good quality and, having determined it, we can hardly pass the chance to use it in the detailed solution approach.

The goal is to evaluate more precisely the performance of the workshop, by incorporating the scheduling problems and estimating the makespan. For this purpose, we will make use of the coupling presented in section 10.3. The complete process is shown in Figure 10.6. It consists of two phases that we briefly describe:

– the initialization phase involves solving the aggregated problem and using the assignment proposed by the problem solver to initialize the optimization phase;

– the optimization phase is based on the principle of the metaheuristic GRASP (Greedy Randomized Adaptive Search Procedure) [FEO 95]. Assignments are randomly generated in accordance with the ant colony paradigm (the QAP-optimal solution effectively allows initializing the baseline pheromone rates). These assignments are then evaluated by the ILS/simulation coupling acting as a black box. The appeal of the ant colony approach is the ability to generate assignments which are "neighbors" of that proposed by the problem solver, and to focus in the most promising assignments.

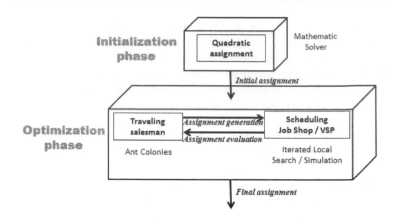

Figure 10.6. *Solution approach for the workshop configuration problem*

The results obtained are shown in Table 10.3. For each of the 40 instances, we show the best assignment that we found with our solution method. We also include the makespan that was obtained for this assignment (column "C_{best}") and the makespan that was obtained for the QAP-optimal assignment (column "C_{QAP}"). Results show that in 17 of 40 cases, taking into account a more precise model helps to propose an assignment other than the QAP-optimal solution. Most of the time, gains are relatively small. Nevertheless, there are some configurations with significant differences. This is the case, for example, for instance Ex21 where QAP-optimal solution leads to a 116 makespan, whereas, we found another configuration with a 106 makespan.

We have precisely represented Gantt charts of these two solutions (Figure 10.7). These charts include a great deal of information:

– transports made by vehicles are represented differently for loaded travels, unloaded travels and idle periods. We indicate the origin machine, the destination machine and the part transported in loaded travels;

– the operations of each machine are shown by specifying the processed part and the order of the operation in the range;

– for every solution, the sum of idle periods of the vehicles and the sum of traveling times with or without load are given.

We note that the QAP-optimal solution minimizes the sum of all the loaded travel times. We find a 144 value (which agrees with results shown in Table 10.2) as compared with 150 for the solution proposed. The difference is clear for the unloaded travels (80 versus 58). This second solution is clearly better that the optimal solution, and justifies the value of the procedure.

Instances	Best Assign	C_{best}	C_{QAP}	Instances	Best Assign	C_{best}	C_{QAP}
Ex11	(2,4,LU,1,3)	98	98	Ex61	(3,4,LU,2,1)	123	129
Ex12	(LU,1,3,4,2)	82	84	Ex62	(LU,1,2,3,4)	102	102
Ex13	(LU,3,4,1,2)	91	92	Ex63	(LU,1,2,3,4)	105	105
Ex14	(4,1,2,LU,3)	114	119	Ex64	(1,2,3,LU,4)	132	135
Ex21	(3,4,LU,2,1)	106	116	Ex71	(2,3,4,LU,1)	124	124
Ex22	(LU,1,2,3,4)	82	86	Ex72	(LU,1,2,3,4)	86	86
Ex23	(LU,1,2,3,4)	89	89	Ex73	(LU,1,2,3,4)	93	93
Ex24	(1,2,3,LU,4)	118	120	Ex74	(1,2,3,LU,4)	138	141
Ex31	(4,1,LU,2,3)	114	117	Ex81	(LU,1,2,3,4)	167	167
Ex32	(1,2,3,4,LU)	89	89	Ex82	(LU,1,2,3,4)	155	155
Ex33	(LU,1,2,3,4)	96	96	Ex83	(LU,1,2,3,4)	155	155
Ex34	(1,2,3,LU,4)	121	121	Ex84	(1,2,3,LU,4)	165	165
Ex41	(1,3,2,LU,4)	123	123	Ex91	(1,2,4,LU,3)	115	115
Ex42	(3,LU,4,1,2)	94	94	Ex92	(LU,3,1,2,4)	97	99
Ex43	(LU,1,2,3,4)	102	102	Ex93	(1,2,4,LU,3)	101	101
Ex44	(1,2,3,LU,4)	140	142	Ex94	(1,4,3,LU,2)	125	126
Ex51	(3,2,4,LU,1)	94	97	Ex101	(4,LU,2,1,3)	148	153
Ex52	(2,LU,3,4,1)	73	74	Ex102	(LU,2,1,3,4)	132	132
Ex53	(4,1,2,LU,3)	81	81	Ex103	(2,1,3,4,LU)	135	135
Ex54	(3,2,4,LU,1)	107	107	Ex104	(2,1,3,LU,4)	158	159

Table 10.3. *Comparison of assignments – makespan criterion*

10.5. Conclusion

The purpose of this study was to show the value that could represent the exploitation of scheduling to solve the machine assignment problem in the workshop.

Results show that, in certain cases, the optimal solution provided by the high-level aggregated model was sometimes challenged by the more precise model, and sometimes with significant productivity gains.

The main flaw of this work is that sometimes it requires the application of a complex solution procedure. In the present case, the proposed method combined hybridization and coupling techniques at the same time.

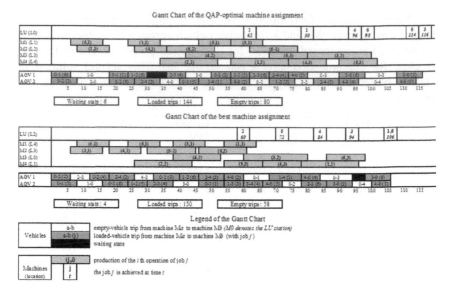

Figure 10.7. *Gantt Chart [DER 13]*

Synchronization Problems
Based on Vehicle Routings

The idea of connecting two problems of a supply chain is not new. Some problems have been studied since the 1980s. More recently, there is a growing conviction that Operational Research has had enough progress to process such problems effectively. These advances are certainly technological, but they are also methodological due to the development of increasingly efficient methods (linear solvers, metaheuristics, etc).

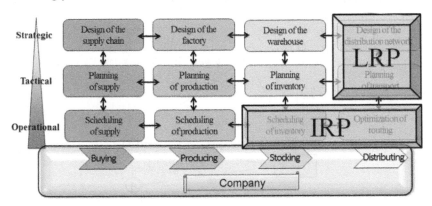

Figure 11.1. *Positioning of inventory and of location routing problems in supply chain management*

We are going to present two problems well identified in the literature. They are both built around vehicle routing problems. The first one is an inventory routing problem (IRP). The second one is a location routing problem (LRP). The IRP is a horizontal synchronization problem that implements the storage and distribution activities at the operational level. The LRP is, in turn, a problem of vertical synchronization between the strategic level for site location and the tactical level for the routing. It plays a role in the design and dimensioning of the distribution network. The mapping of these problems is shown in Figure 11.1.

11.1. Inventory routing problem

11.1.1. *Presentation of the problem*

11.1.1.1. *Introductory example*

The IRP is an old one. One of the historical papers on the subject is [BEL 83]. The authors introduced stock management for the elaboration of vehicle routings in the field of industrial gas distribution. To illustrate the impact and importance of inventory inclusion, they use the example described below.

Let us take four customers, each having a different tank capacity and their own daily needs. The company has a deposit and a vehicle with a capacity of 5,000 gal[1], which can make two trips a day. The data set of the problem is shown in Figure 11.2.

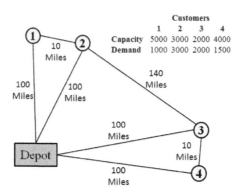

Figure 11.2. *A historical example of the IRP [BEL 83]*

---

1 The gallon (gal) is an Anglo-Saxon volume unit. 1 gal GB = 4.54609 liters and 1 gal US = 3.785411784 liters.

An obvious solution is to make two trips a day. In the first trip, the vehicle delivers 1,000 gal to customer 1 and 3,000 to customer 2. In the course of the second trip, it delivers to customers 3 and 4 2,000 and 1,500, respectively. The total distance traveled each day is $2 \times 210 = 420$ miles. Both routings comply with the capacity of the vehicle.

However, the previous solution is not the best one. Let us assume that the vehicle makes different deliveries from one day to the other. The first day, it delivers to customers 1 and 2, but only delivers 2,000 gal to customer 1 (assuming a demand coverage equal to two days). With the 3,000 gal delivered to customer 2, the vehicle is full. On the same day, it delivers in the same fashion to customers 3 and 4 but delivering 3,000 gal to customer 4 and consistently 2,000 gal to customer 3. On the second day, customers 1 and 4 have enough stock so as not to need another delivery. The vehicle only completes one routing in which it delivers 3,000 gal to customer 2 and 2,000 gal to customer 3 for a total distance traveled of 340 miles in the second day, instead of the 420 miles from the previous solution.

Through this example and the analysis of the second solution, we clearly observe the issue of coverage of demand, and thus, of delivery frequency for each customer. This has a direct influence on all clients that will receive a delivery daily, and has a strong impact on routing organization.

In this example, only transport costs are taken into account. Very often, inventory costs are also integrated to the evaluation of the solution.

11.1.1.2. *Linear program of the IRP*

We present a classical model of this problem, proposed by Archetti *et al.* [ARC 07] (Box 11.1). The authors analyzed a logistic network in which the single depot (or supplier in the article), numbered 0, distributes to n customers (or retailers) and is represented by the set $M = \{1, \dots, n\}$. The horizon T is divided into H periods. On each period $t \in T$, an additional quantity $r_{0,t}$ of goods arrive in the depot and the customer demand is equal to $r_{s,t}$, $\forall s \in M$. The supplier has an initial stock B_0. Each customer also has an initial stock $I_{s,0}$ and a storage capacity U_s. In the reorder policy applied, when a customer is visited, the delivered amount $x_{s,t}$ is defined so that the customer's stock reaches its maximal value U_s (then we have $x_{s,t} = U_s - I_{s,t}$).

Data:

$M' = M \cup \{0\}$: all customers plus the depot

$T = \{1,...,H\}$: horizon broken down in periods

$r_{0,t}$: quantity received in the depot during period $t \in T$

$r_{s,t}$: customer demand $s \in M$ for the period $t \in T$

B_0 : initial stock in the depot

$I_{s,0}$: initial stock of the customer $s \in M$

U_s : storage capacity of the client $s \in M$

h_0 : storage unit cost in the depot

h_s : storage unit cost for the customer $s \in M$

C : capacity of the vehicle

$c_{ij}, i,j \in M'$: transport cost among the nodes i and j

Variables:

$$y_{i,j}^t = \begin{cases} 1 \text{ if } i \text{ precedes } j \text{ at period } t \\ 0 \text{ otherwise} \end{cases}, \forall (i,j) \in M' \otimes M', \forall t \in T$$

$x_{s,t}$: quantity of goods delivered to the customer $s \in M$ for period $t \in T$

$$z_{s,t} = \begin{cases} 1 \text{ if the customer } s \text{ is delivered at period } t \\ 0 \text{ otherwise} \end{cases}, \forall s \in M, \forall t \in T$$

$$z_{0,t} = \begin{cases} 1 \text{ if the depot delivers at least one customer at period } t \\ 0 \text{ otherwise} \end{cases}, \forall t \in T$$

B_t : stock level of the depot during period $t \in T$

$I_{s,t}$: stock level of the customer $s \in M$ during period $t \in T$

Minimize:

$$h_0 \sum_{t \in T'} B_t + \sum_{s \in M}\left(h_s \times \sum_{t \in T'} I_{s,t} \right) + \sum_{i \in M'} \sum_{j \in M', i<j} \sum_{t \in T} c_{i,j} y_{i,j}^t \qquad [11.1]$$

Under the constraints

$$B_t = B_{t-1} + r_{0,t-1} - \sum_{s \in M} x_{s,t-1}, \forall t \in T' \text{ (with } r_{0,0} = x_{s,0} = 0) \qquad [11.2]$$

$$B_t \geq \sum_{s \in M} x_{s,t}, \forall t \in T \qquad [11.3]$$

$$I_{s,t} = I_{s,t-1} + x_{s,t-1} - r_{s,t-1}, \forall s \in M, \forall t \in T' \text{ (with } r_{s,0} = x_{s,0} = 0) \qquad [11.4]$$

$$I_{s,t} \geq 0, \forall s \in S, \forall t \in T' \qquad [11.5]$$

$$x_{s,t} \geq U_s z_{s,t} - I_{s,t}, \forall s \in M, \forall t \in T \qquad [11.6]$$

$$x_{s,t} \leq U_s - I_{s,t}, \forall s \in M, \forall t \in T \qquad [11.7]$$

$$x_{s,t} \leq U_s z_{s,t}, \forall s \in S, \forall t \in T \qquad [11.8]$$

$$\sum_{s\in M} x_{s,t} \le C, \forall t \in T \qquad\qquad [11.9]$$

$$\sum_{s\in M} x_{s,t} \le C \times z_{0,t}, \forall t \in T \qquad\qquad [11.10]$$

$$\sum_{j\in M',j>i} y'_{i,j} + \sum_{j\in M',j<i} y'_{j,i} \le 2z_{i,t}, \forall i \in M', \forall t \in T \qquad [11.11]$$

$$\sum_{i\in S}\sum_{j\in S,i<j} y'_{i,j} \le \sum_{i\in S} z_{i,t} - z_{k,t}, \forall k \in S \subseteq M, \forall t \in T \qquad [11.12]$$

Box 11.1. *Linear program of the inventory routing problem*

The objective function [11.1] is the sum of three terms. Inventory costs are calculated at depot and customer level. If B_t is the level of the depot inventory during the period $t \in T$ and if h_0 is the inventory unit cost, the total inventory cost of the depot is equal to $h_0 \times \sum_{t\in T'} B_t$ where $T' = T \cup \{H+1\}$ (a period is added to the horizon to take into account the decisions taken during the last period). Likewise, if h_s is the inventory unit cost of the customer s, the total inventory cost of that customer is equal to $h_s \times \sum_{t\in T'} I_{s,t}$.

A vehicle with C capacity performs a distribution routing. $c_{i,j}$ represents the transportation cost to go from i to j, $\forall(i,j)\in[M']^2$ (the costs are assumed to be symmetrical: $c_{i,j} = c_{j,i}$).

We try to determine then the amounts delivered by customer and by period $x_{s,t}$. Variables $y'_{i,j}$ have a value of one if the node i (depot or customer) precedes node j in the routing of period t. Variables B_t and $I_{s,t}$ are integers that represent quantities of goods in stock inside the depot or with the customers. Finally, variables $z_{s,t}$ indicate whether the customer is given service for a period and eventually if the depot is used for a period (if it is not used, there will be no deliveries for any clients).

Constraints [11.2] are stock balance constraints for the depot. Constraints [11.3] require that in each period, the quantity in stock at the depot is enough to supply customers. Constraints [11.4] are stock balance constraints for each customer. Constraints [11.5] forbid stock-outs in the customer facilities.

Constraints [11.6]–[11.8] ensure the implementation of the required policy for supply management. They use variables $z_{s,t}$ to linearize the expression of this policy. If $z_{s,t} = 1$, we will have $x_{s,t} = U_s - I_{s,t}$ by constraints [11.6] and [11.7], otherwise $x_{s,t} = 0$ by constraint [11.8]. Constraints [11.9] guarantee that the vehicle capacity is respected. Constraints [11.10]–[11.12] are routing-related constraints. Constraints [11.10] require that a trip leaves from the depots as soon as a customer receives a delivery during the period. Constraints [11.11] say that every customer in a tour has a predecessor and a successor. Constraints [11.12] are elimination constraints of sub cycles.

Andersson *et al.* [AND 10] and Coelho *et al.* [COE 13] propose a state-of-the-art on the IRP; there are two excellent readings for those who want to broaden their knowledge on the subject.

11.1.2. *Resolution by metaheuristics*

Many metaheuristic-based approaches have been proposed to solve the IRP. We describe some that show their diversity, both in hybridization techniques, and in the choice of the metaheuristic that has been applied.

Campbell and Savelsbergh [CAM 04] describe a decomposition approach where the problem is broken down into two subproblems that are solved sequentially. The first subproblem involves the planning of distribution with a daily bucket. The aim is to identify customers that will receive deliveries each day and in what quantities. This subproblem is modeled as a linear integer programming and is solved to optimality. The result is used as a guide for the second subproblem, which is the organization of distribution routings. The resulting issue is a vehicle-routing problem with time windows (VRP-TW) which can be solved with a GRASP-type metaheuristic. The authors propose two instances: one with 50 customers and another with 100 customers. They work with a horizon that stretches four weeks.

Archetti *et al.* [ARC 12] propose hybridization between a metaheuristic and an exact method. The authors use a classic scheme with a tabu search where the exploration of a big neighborhood is implemented. For that purpose, the authors rely on the solution of two mixed linear programs that are solved in an optimal way if the size of the instances allows it. If this is not the case, a time limit is set. The cases processed have 60 customers and work over 6 periods.

Moi *et al.* [MOI 11] use the multi-product variant of the IRP. They propose two variants of a hybrid genetic algorithm according to the coding used to represent a solution. They adopt an integrated approach. A chromosome is either a binary matrix that indicates in which periods customers are supplied, or an integer matrix that represents the quantities to be delivered. The instances processed have 98 customers over 14 periods.

Mjirda *et al.* [MIJ 14] address again the previous problem. They describe a hybrid metaheuristic in two phases. In the first phase, the authors solve the vehicle routing problem by neglecting the stock management. They propose a variable neighborhood search (VNS). The result obtained is used as initial solution for the second phase that integrates the inventory costs. A search and a variable neighborhood descent (VND) are then proposed to improve the solution.

11.2. The location-routing problem

The LRP synchronizes the location problem and the vehicle routing problem. This is a problem that has grown significantly in recent years and has become an important logistic issue.

11.2.1. *Definition of the problem*

The LRP problem is shown in Figure 11.3. This problem covers three phases that are explained in the figure. Given a set of potential sites (warehouses in this case), phase 1 involves choosing which ones will be exploited (here warehouses three, four and six represented with a grey-colored spot). For phase 2, a set of customers is considered, possibly with a demand to be satisfied. Each customer is then assigned to a warehouse which will be responsible for servicing him, respecting capacity constraints on the warehouses. In phase 3, routings are organized for each warehouse, respecting capacity constraints on vehicles. The goal is to perform these three phases while minimizing the sum of the costs, for instance, operating costs of warehouses, fixed costs per vehicle and transportation costs.

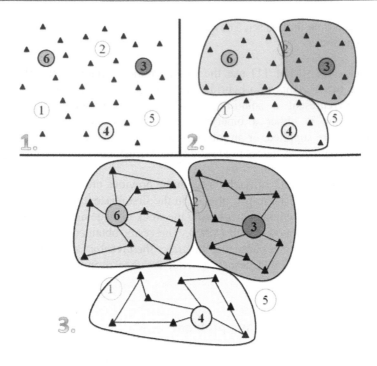

Figure 11.3. *The three phases of the "Location Routing Problem"*

In recent years, this problem has been increasingly studied. Nagy and Salhi [NAG 07] have proposed a first state-of-the-art, recently completed by Prodhon and Prins [PRO 14]. In this paper, the authors identify 72 articles that have been dedicated to the matter between 2007 and 2014, showing its dynamism. Cuda *et al.* [CUD 15] prepared a state-of-the-art report dedicated to the two-step supply chains. Finally, Drexl and Schneider [DRE 15] prepared a classification of the different variants of the LRP. In their opinion, the main characteristics are:

– *deterministic/stochastic/fuzzy data*: this category characterizes the nature of the data, depending on whether they are deterministic, in the form of a probability distribution or fuzzy numbers;

– *statistical/dynamic/periodical problems*: static problems characterize mono-period problems (those whose structure is not expected to evolve over time). The other issues are multi-period problems. In periodical problems, it is assumed that all data are known in advance. The aim of periodic problems is to decide the periods in which to visit each customer;

– *discrete/continuous locations*: depending on whether the sites can be selected from a predetermined set of potential sites or sites can be located freely on a map;

– *single/multi echelon*: depending on whether the levels are taken into account or not in a distribution chain. In a single-echelon problem, the only distributors taken into account are those who directly supply customers. Otherwise, producers or providers can also be included in the study;

– *single/multi objective*: often, the minimization criterion of the cost sum is used. Some works also include qualitative criteria such as quality of service;

– *node/arc routing*: depending on whether the service is to be performed on the nodes of the graph or on the arcs.

One feature that does not appear in this classification is to include or not capacity constraints, either for the vehicle or the warehouses. Taking them into consideration can help to cope with dimensioning issues of the vehicle fleet, something that we consider important at this level of decision-making.

We decided to introduce the linear program shown in Box 11.2 [PRI 07]. It is a variant of the classic LRP with deterministic data, a static problem, discrete locations, a single-echelon approach, a single-objective approach, node routings and capacity planning.

The objective of this model is to minimize the sum of the warehouse operating cost, the vehicle fixed costs and the transportation costs [11.13]. Constraints [11.14] ensure that all customers are supplied. Constraints [11.15] guarantee capacity constraints of the vehicles. Constraints [11.16] and [11.17] maintain route coherence and force vehicles to return to the depot they departed from. Constraints [11.18] are the elimination constraints of sub cycles. The constraints [11.19] state that if there is a route between a warehouse and a client, then the client is assigned to the warehouse. Finally, constraints [11.20] are capacity constraints of the warehouses.

Data:

$I = \{1,...,n\}$: set of potential warehouses

$J = \{1,...,m\}$: set of customers

$V = I \cup J$: set of graph vertices

$W_i, i \in I$: warehouse capacity

$O_i, i \in I$: warehouse operating costs

$d_j, j \in J$: customer demand

$c_{ij}, i \in I, j \in J$: transportation cost between warehouses and customers

$K = \{1,...,k\}$: set of vehicles

C : vehicle capacity (homogeneous fleet)

F : fixed cost of a vehicle

Variables:

$$y_i = \begin{cases} 1 \text{ if warehouse } i \text{ is open} \\ 0 \text{ otherwise} \end{cases}, \forall i \in I$$

$$f_{ij} = \begin{cases} 1 \text{ if customer } j \text{ receives deliveries from warehouse } i \\ 0 \text{ otherwise} \end{cases}, \forall (i,j) \in I \times J$$

$$x_{ijk} = \begin{cases} 1 \text{ if vehicle } k \text{ travels the arc } (i,j) \\ 0 \text{ otherwise} \end{cases}, \forall (i,j) \in (I \cup J)^2$$

Minimize:

$$\sum_{i \in I} O_i y_i + \sum_{i \in V} \sum_{j \in V} \left(c_{ij} \sum_{k \in K} x_{ijk} \right) + F \sum_{k \in K} \sum_{i \in I} \sum_{j \in J} x_{ijk} \qquad [11.13]$$

Under the constraints

$$\sum_{k \in K} \sum_{i \in V} x_{ijk} = 1, \forall j \in J \qquad [11.14]$$

$$\sum_{i \in V} \sum_{j \in J} d_j x_{ijk} \le Q, \forall k \in K \qquad [11.15]$$

$$\sum_{j \in V} x_{ijk} - \sum_{j \in V} x_{jik} = 0, \forall i \in V, \forall k \in K \qquad [11.16]$$

$$\sum_{i \in I} \sum_{j \in J} x_{ijk} \le 1, \forall k \in K \qquad [11.17]$$

$$\sum_{i \in S} \sum_{j \in S} x_{ijk} \le |S| - 1, \forall S \subset J, \forall k \in K \qquad [11.18]$$

$$\sum_{u \in J} x_{iuk} + \sum_{u \in V \setminus \{j\}} x_{ujk} \le 1 + f_{ij}, \forall i \in I, \forall j \in J, \forall k \in K \qquad [11.19]$$

$$\sum_{j \in J} d_j f_{ij} \le W_i y_i, \forall i \in I \qquad [11.20]$$

Box 11.2. *Linear program of location routing problem*

11.2.2. *Solution with metaheuristics*

As in the case of the IRP, we focus on a few works of the literature that make use of metaheuristics.

Doulabi and Seifi [DOU 13] deal with a variant in which routing takes place on an arc. The capacity of vehicles is taken into account. By contrast, warehouses, strictly speaking, do not have a capacity. However, the number of routings that can be associated with them is increased. The authors propose a low-level hybrid method in which a simulated annealing works on partial solutions. Solutions are completed with a two-phase approach: first, a savings-type heuristic that merges short routings followed by a second heuristic that allocates routings to warehouses.

Derbel *et al.* [DER 12] propose a hybrid method in which they combine a genetic algorithm (GA) with an iterated local search (ILS). The procedure is similar to a memetic algorithm where local search is replaced by the ILS. They adopt an integrated approach representing a solution with two vectors; the first one indicates the warehouse to which the customer has been assigned, and a second one that establishes the position of the client in the route.

Ting and Chen [TIN 13] propose a hybrid method based on a multi-level ant colony. They break down the classic LRP problem into three subproblems and apply, on each one, an ant-colony algorithm. Each colony is applied iteratively until a stopping criterion is found. The three subproblems are:

– warehouse location;

– assignment of customers to warehouses;

– elaboration of routings.

Duhamel *et al.* [DUH 11] use a hybrid GRASP/ELS method. Local search in GRASP is replaced by an evolution of the iterated local search "*Evolutionary Local Search*" capable of generating several solutions with one iteration each. The originality of this problem-solving approach lies in working on two search areas: a classical LRP solution and a giant tour that is obtained by concatenating the routings and eliminating depots.

There are many other approaches. The latest state-of-the-art that we have mentioned will help to explore them in more detail. What is interesting is the diversity of approaches used. Almost every metaheuristic, whether individual or population-based, is successfully applied on this difficult problem.

11.3. Conclusion

To conclude this section, we have focused on two logistical problems that act as the interface between different actors or activities. Both problems have been studied for many years and are well documented as we could show it through our brief overview. There are similar problems. Among them, we can mention the *"Production Routing Problem"* (PRP) [ADU 15], which synchronizes lot-sizing problems and vehicle routings; even the *"Location-Inventory-Routing Problem"* that combines our two problems and which has a few references in the literature.

The resolution of such problems has required and still requires significant methodological efforts, with a need to move toward hybridization techniques that rely on even more sophisticated and better controlled methods. Answers begin to be put forward but many things remain to be done. Synchronization issues, the ones that we have discussed and all the others, are part of the supply chain management, with many research opportunities for the years to come.

Solution to Problems

In this final chapter, we return to the small problems outlined at the beginning of this book.

12.1. The swing state problem

1. *What kind of combinatorial optimization problem is the "swing state" problem in relation with?*

The candidate has an overall budget of $ 500 k, comparable to a capacity C. He must, therefore, choose which states he must invest in, knowing that each state $i \in I$ has a value v_i, which corresponds to the number of voters that he will bring in, and a cost m_i. The objective is to maximize the summation of the value of all the chosen states, without exceeding the capacity. We can recognize the knapsack problem.

2. *Determine a criterion according to which the states can be ranked from most interesting to least interesting. Deduce a construction heuristic from this and give its principle. What solution do you find?*

We will define as a saturated solution one for which it is not possible to add new states without violating the capacity constraint. The purpose of this question is to find a criterion that helps to sort states out. The order thus defined will allow determining which states will be selected through a greedy heuristic.

Three sorting criteria can be proposed:

– prioritizing states that require smaller investments (cost criterion);

– prioritizing states that give the most electoral votes (value criterion);

– prioritizing states where the investment per electoral vote obtained is the largest (ratio criterion).

The last criterion seems clearly the more relevant because it is the only one that takes into account both the cost and value of each state. The principle of the greedy heuristic algorithm is shown in Box 12.1. The mistake that students often make is stopping the algorithm whenever the integration of a state entails a capacity overflow. It is of course necessary to continue (hence, the loop for in the principle algorithm) to saturate the solution. This consideration does not apply to the cost criterion, as states are arranged in order of increasing cost. If a state is too costly, the following are necessarily so.

In Table 13.1, we indicate for each state if they were selected or not by the greedy heuristic according to the three criteria indicated, and include in the column value the number of electoral votes won in each case. Unsurprisingly, we notice that the ratio criterion provides the best result with 83 electoral votes. This last solution needs an investment of $ 480 k.

Function *Greedy Heuristic* $(m : array, v : array, C : integer, n : integer)$

    Dim *Sum* : integer

    Dim *i* : integer

    Dim σ : array

    Dim *Solution* : array

    $Sum \leftarrow 0$

    Initialize σ according to the chosen criteria (cost, value or ratio)

    For *i* **from** 1 **to** *n* **Do**

        If $Sum + m(\sigma(i)) \leq C$ **then**

            $Solution(\sigma(i)) = 1$

            $Sum = Sum + m(\sigma(i))$

        Otherwise

            $Solution(\sigma(i)) = 0$

        End If

    End For

    Return *Solution*

End Function

Box 12.1. *Principle of greedy heuristics to construct a solution*

Swing states	Cost criterion	Value	Value criterion	Value	Ratio criterion	Value
Colorado	1	9	0	0	1	9
Florida	0	0	1	27	0	0
Indiana	1	11	0	0	1	11
Missouri	0	0	0	0	0	0
New Hampshire	1	4	0	0	1	4
New Mexico	1	5	0	0	0	0
Nevada	1	5	1	5	0	0
North Carolina	1	15	0	0	1	15
Ohio	0	0	1	20	0	0
Pennsylvania	0	0	1	21	1	21
Virginia	1	13	0	0	1	13
Wisconsin	1	10	0	0	1	10
Number of electoral votes		72		73		83

Table 12.1. *Results of the greedy heuristic in accordance with the criteria*

3. Remove the most expensive state from the last solution. Can you then complete your solution by choosing some other states, thus improving it?

We will use the resulting solution with the criterion ratio. By removing the state of Pennsylvania and its 21 electoral votes, there is $ 130 k to be distributed among the remaining five states (Florida, Missouri, New Mexico, Nevada and Ohio). This subproblem can be solved in an optimal way by a simple enumeration, especially when Florida and Ohio are outside the budget. By investing in Missouri and Nevada ($ 120 k for 16 electoral votes), we obtain a new solution that unfortunately is both more expensive ($ 490 k against 480) and gives less (78 electoral votes against 83).

4. Deduce a neighborhood system for this problem.

Let I^+ be the set of states chosen and I^- be its complementary. A simple neighborhood system is to select randomly one (or several) states of I^+ which will be removed from the solution and replaced by one or several states of I^-, which will be chosen in several ways:

– by choosing randomly one or several states of I^-, until the constructed solution is saturated. This technique will be all the more effective as the number of states removed is very small (one or two);

– by solving the problem thus obtained in an optimal way. The number of states removed must be such that this resolution is possible. The idea is to be able to exploit a large neighborhood. If an exact solution is not possible, an approximate method (such as the greedy heuristic for example) can also be implemented to saturate the solution.

Note that ejection chain techniques can also be developed.

5. *Propose the most appropriate upper and lower bounds of the optimal solution*

Let x^* be an optimal solution. It is already established that $H(x^*) \geq 83$. We only have to obtain an upper bound for enclosing $H(x^*)$. This value can be obtained by reasoning in terms of the ratio criterion. According to this criterion, the first six states are, respectively, Pennsylvania, North Carolina, Florida, Missouri and New Hampshire. This unsaturated solution costs \$ 450 k for 79 electoral votes. The next state in the list is Missouri that costs \$80 k and gets 11 electoral votes. If we could make a partial investment in this state up to \$50 k, that would give us 6.875 electoral votes. With the remaining amount, it is not possible to expect better than 6 electoral votes, having an upper bound of 85 electoral votes.

We then obtain the enclosed range $83 \leq H(x^*) \leq 85$.

It is easy to notice that by completing the six previous states with Nevada instead of New Hampshire, we obtain a solution that costs \$490 k and brings in 84 electoral votes. The use of a solver for this problem shows that this is an optimal solution.

12.2. Adel and his camels

12.2.1. *First question*

This question concerns the two-machine flow-shop problem. It is very simple provided, of course, that you know the Johnson rule and have understood the difference between the P and NP class problems.

What kind of optimization problem has Mr L. recognized? And why does he seem so happy?

Of course, Mr L. has recognized the flow-shop problem. From his jovial mood, we can deduce he knows that the two-machine problem with makespan minimization is polynomial, and that he knows the method to solve the problem.

What solving technique is Mr L. going to employ?

Mr L. is going to rely on the Johnson rule to solve this problem (section 6.2.1.1). Let I denote all the camels and $p_{i,j}$ the preparation times of camels for $1 \le i \le 12$ and $1 \le j \le 2$. The method involves constructing the sets $U = \{i \in I \mid p_{i,1} < p_{i,2}\}$ and $V = \{i \in I \mid p_{i,1} \ge p_{i,2}\}$. We have $U = \{2,4,6,7,8,10,11\}$ and $V = \{1,3,5,9,12\}$. These sets are sorted out according to $p_{i,1}$ in increasing order for U and according to $p_{i,2}$ in decreasing order for V. We obtain ordered lists $(7,8,11,2,6,10,4)$ and $(5,12,1,9,3)$. Their concatenation provides an optimal permutation $\sigma = (7,8,11,2,6,10,4,5,12,1,9,3)$ to the problem.

What will the tourists' waiting time be?

It is sufficient to evaluate the previous permutation through a Gantt chart (Figure 12.1). Camels will be ready at 10:06, which will cause a 6 min wait for tourists. Whether Adel finds this too long or not, it cannot be reduced.

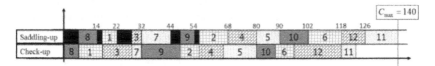

Figure 12.1. *Gantt chart of a scheduling obtained with the Johnson rule*

12.2.2. Second question

The tourists now arrive in small groups. The aim is to ensure that camels are always ready for the arrival of a group, which makes the problem slightly more difficult!

He thanks you heartily for determining the order in which the camels have to be geared up and starts calculating the sum of all the tourists' waiting times. What number will Adel find?

The permutation obtained in the previous question minimizes the preparation times for the entire set of camels. Adel thinks that this solution is similarly adapted to this new situation. Table 12.2 simply allows determining the sum of tourists' waiting times. We indicate in the line "Camel" the time in which camels are ready (values that can be directly read on Gantt chart), in the columns "Arrival" and "Departure", respectively, the tourists' arrival time and departure time for a hike, and finally in the "Standby" column the waiting time of each tourist is given. The cumulative sum of delays is equal to 36 min. We refer to this case as "isolated departures" as opposed to the case of "grouped departures" that appears in the following question.

Tourists	A	B	C	D	E	F	G	H	I	J	K	L
Camels	8h16	8h24	8h38	8h50	9h04	9h16	9h28	9h38	9h48	9h54	10h00	10h06
Arrival	8h30	8h30	8h30	9h00	9h00	9h00	9h30	9h30	10h00	10h00	10h00	10h10
Departure	8h38	8h38	8h38	9h16	9h16	9h16	9h38	9h38	10h00	10h00	10h00	10h10
Delay (min)	-	-	8	-	4	16	-	8	-	-	-	-

Table 12.2. *Evaluation of delays (case of isolated departures)*

The situation is even worse than Adel thought... What is the actual overall waiting time?

Tourists, therefore, expect that enough camels are ready to leave in groups. The correction is featured in Table 12.3. The cumulative sum of delays is much more important for it is 88 min long.

Tourists	A	B	C	D	E	F	G	H	I	J	K	L
Camels	8h16	8h24	8h38	8h50	9h04	9h16	9h28	9h38	9h48	9h54	10h00	10h06
Arrival	8h30	8h30	8h30	9h00	9h00	9h00	9h30	9h30	10h00	10h00	10h00	10h10
Departure	8h38	8h38	8h38	9h16	9h16	9h16	9h38	9h38	10h00	10h00	10h00	10h10
Delay (min)	8	8	8	16	16	16	8	8	-	-	-	-

Table 12.3. *Evaluation of delays (case of grouped departures)*

Adel puts forward the idea that the camels more readily available should be favored. .... Describe and then employ a greedy heuristic procedure in relation to this idea. Will this solution satisfy Adel?

Let us call dd_i (per date due) the customer arrival time i . The criterion to be minimized is no longer the makespan but the sum of delays. In the first case, this criterion can be expressed as $\sum_{i \in I} \max\left(t_{\sigma(i),2} - dd_i, 0\right)$, with $t_{\sigma(i),j}$

the completion time for the preparation i^{th} camel for the operation j, Supposedly, customers are numbered according to their date of arrival. This criterion must be slightly adapted to take into account the constraint of grouped departures. The difficulty lies in the fact that this two-machine flow-shop is no longer a polynomial problem [LEN 77], which justifies the use of heuristic procedures.

The heuristic proposed by Adel incorporates the idea of the nearest neighbor heuristic from the TSP (section 5.2.1). This is a greedy method that involves choosing camels one after the other by giving priority to the one that will be ready earlier. The principle of this heuristic is shown in Box 12.2.

Initialize I all the camels
$\sigma = \varnothing$
While $I \neq \varnothing$ **Do**
    For $i \in I$ **Do**
        Evaluate the sum of delays of $\sigma \circ (i)$
    End For
    Choose i^* the camel that minimizes the sum of delays
    $I \leftarrow I \setminus \{i^*\}$
    $\sigma \leftarrow \sigma \circ (i^*)$
End While

Box 12.2. *Principle algorithm of greedy heuristics*

The solution constructed using this heuristic is represented in the Gantt chart of Figure 12.2. We can note a constant downtime for saddling, which results in a relatively high makespan (140 instead of 126 for an optimal makespan). The sum of delays is 58 min, which is better than the initial solution (Table 12.4). The effect of the heuristic is, therefore, significant even if the result is relatively deceiving (we will see in the next question that it is possible to do much better)

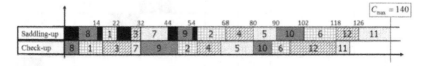

Figure 12.2. *Gantt chart of the greedy heuristic solution*

Tourists	A	B	C	D	E	F	G	H	I	J	K	L
Camels	8h14	8h22	8h32	8h44	8h54	9h08	9h20	9h30	9h42	9h58	10h06	10h20
Arrival	8h30	8h30	8h30	9h00	9h00	9h00	9h30	9h30	10h00	10h00	10h00	10h10
Departure	8h32	8h32	8h32	9h08	9h08	9h08	9h30	9h30	10h06	10h06	10h06	10h20
Delay (min)	2	2	2	8	8	8	0	0	6	6	6	10

Table 12.4. *Evaluation of the greedy heuristic solution*

12.2.3. *Third question*

Adel, discouraged, turns once again to Mr L. In your opinion, how will the story end?

We finish this exercise with an open question that often puzzles students. It is not the answer that it is evaluated but the reasoning that leads to that answer. The fact to propose a heuristic, to apply it and to conclude that the end of the story will be negative is just as valid as trying to build a solution that does not include any delay and to find one. Know that such solutions exist, including at least one that keeps an optimal makespan of 126. Will you know how to find it?

12.3. The forges of Sauron

12.3.1. *The inspection of the forges*

1. Fill out the distance in Table 1.4 ... Why is it not necessary to provide information about every case presented in this chart?

	M	1	2	3	4	5	6	7	8	9	10	11
M		7	3	4	9	6	8	12	9	13	7	10
1			4	11	16	5	7	11	10	15	13	16
2				7	12	4	6	10	9	14	10	13
3					5	10	9	8	5	9	3	6
4						12	11	10	7	10	4	7
5							2	6	5	10	8	11
6								4	4	8	7	11
7									3	4	6	7
8										7	3	6
9											6	3
10												3
11												

Table 12.5. *Transit times (in hours) between two sites*

The chart will make calculations easier for the rest of the exercise. It is obtained by finding the shortest path on the Mordor map. Since the graph is not oriented, the distance does not depend on the route direction and the matrix is symmetric. Let us note that triangle inequality is satisfied.

2. What is the name of the problem you have to solve? What solution do you obtain when you apply the "nearest neighbor" heuristic upon leaving the mine? .... Can you hope to obtain a better result if you apply the same technique but with a different starting point?

The cited problem is that of the traveling salesman. By applying the nearest neighbor heuristic from the mine, the next solution is built: $(M ,2,1,5,6,7,8,10,3,4,11,9,5, M)$ for a total time of 58 h. Applying this construction scheme from any forge allows us to build a different solution. We therefore have every chance to improve the solution by repeating the heuristics as many times as there are sites (the mine plus the forges).

3. Propose the best solution possible.

By taking a closer look at forge eight, all others have a peripheral location. A trip $(M ,2,1,5,6,7,9,11,10,4,3, M)$, therefore, seems very interesting. The only remaining issue is to insert forge eight in this partial solution. The shortest detour (3 h) is obtained by inserting it between forges six and seven. We then obtain the solution $(M ,2,1,5,6,8,7,9,11,10,4,3, M)$ with a travel time equal to 44 h, a lot better than that obtained with the heuristic.

4. Besides inspecting the forges, you want to carry out the delivery of iron. ... Without taking into account the delay on the transport time, what is this problem called? If you retrieve the best solution you found in the last part just as it is, how long will your travel time be?

Without taking into account the penalty on transportation times, we recognize here the VRP problem (section 3.4.2). The mine plays the role of the depot, the forges are the customers and we have capacity constraints to respect.

There are several ways to adapt the solution proposed in question three to integrate these capacity constraints. The goal is to obtain the best possible solution. It is then convenient to take into account the following elements:

– At what time(s) do you decide to interrupt the current tour to return to the mine for resupplying?

– If time penalties are applied, an asymmetry appears when calculating the routing duration and it becomes necessary to consider the direction of travel.

A quick calculation of the amount of iron to be distributed suggested that two routings are required (the sum of the volumes is equal to 160 m³); this will be, a *priori*, sufficient. Any possible penalty on transport time does not justify returning to the mine a second time to resupply for a third routing. It seems reasonable to start from the outset on this assumption.

The first question consists, therefore, of deciding when we will return to the mine. There are only two possibilities that allow respecting capacity constraints. Solution A concerns the first possibility which is returning to the mine after forge seven. Next, operators perform routings $T_A^1 = (M, 2, 1, 5, 6, 8, M)$ and $T_A^2 = (M, 7, 9, 11, 10, 4, 3, M)$ with a respective capacity of 65 and 95. Solution B involves returning to the mine after forge 8. The routings are then $T_B^1 = (M, 2, 1, 5, 6, 8, 7, M)$ and $T_B^2 = (M, 9, 11, 10, 4, 3, M)$. They admit a respective capability of 90 and 70. The durations of all these routings are evaluated in Figure 12.3. On every path followed by the caravan, we indicate the amount of iron that it transports and the duration of the trip. Dark gray boxes indicate a 100% penalty over the duration, while those in light gray indicate a 50% penalty.

Therefore, it will take 78 h in total to complete the two rounds of solution A as compared to 80 h for solution B.

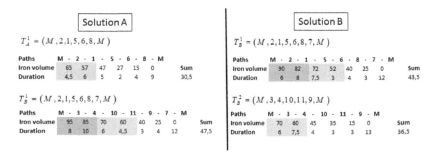

Figure 12.3. *Evaluation of routings*

12.3.2. *Production of the lethal weapon*

Propose an empirical rule (as simple as possible) that can determine a priori where the parts have to be produced. By rigorously applying the rule you have set, what solution do you find? How long will it take you to produce the weapon? Propose an approach that can improve this solution.

This problem consists of synchronizing the production and transportation of parts. In accordance to what we have mentioned, particularly in flexible production systems, we could find this difficult. As a matter of fact, it does not happen that way as long as we have a good start.

Let us start by determining a lower bound for our problem. For this, first, there is a production phase. The total cost of production is equal to $40 + 60 + 120 + 100 + 100 + 3 \times 80 + 5 \times 60 = 960$. The overall hourly production capacity is $6 + 8 + 5 + 8 + 7 + 8 + 10 + 5 + 6 + 5 + 10 = 78$. If all forges operate at full capacity and without any downtime, it will then take 960/78 $960/78 \approx 12,3$ h. Then comes the transportation phase. There will be a total of 88 h of transport to be distributed among 11 mines with 8 h of transportation as an average.

We can expect that if everything goes well, all parts will be returned as of 13+8=21 h. This value will serve as a working basis for establishing the schedule (Figure 12.4). On this schedule, the transport times for each forge are shown on the right side of the chart. The time remaining can be used for the production. By recalling the production capacity of each forge, and the potential production time, we easily deduce the production capacity of each Forge (column "Production"). We tried to squeeze in the production of parts in the remaining spaces. By doing this, we note that because of a lack of flexibility, the 21 h solution is undoubtedly not possible. In the schedule proposed, two projectiles are not manufactured.

Forges	Capacity	Production	1	2	3	4	5	6	7	8	9	10	11	12	13	14	15	16	17	18	19	20	21
1	6	84	Axle (80)														TRANSPORT						
2	8	144	Sling (120)																TRANSPORT				
3	5	85	Axle (80)															TRANSPORT					
4	8	96	Axle (80)											TRANSPORT									
5	7	105	Pulley (100)												TRANSPORT								
6	8	104	Counterweight (100)												TRANSPORT								
7	10	90	Lever (60)							TRANSPORT														
8	5	60	Projectile (60)									TRANSPORT												
9	6	48	Chassis (40)					TRANSPORT																
10	5	70	Projectile (60)										TRANSPORT											
11	10	110	Projectile (60)								TRANSPORT													

Figure 12.4. *Construction schedule of the weapon*

Now that the procedure has been shown, we easily find solutions with 23 h (the sling can be produced on forge 6). Forge 2, which will have a production capacity of 160, will be able to manufacture the counterweight and one of the missing projectiles. The other one can be produced on forge 11.

I did not find any solution of 22 h. Is it possible that you can get it? Or maybe can you prove that is not possible? I thus conclude this book leaving a little riddle.

Conclusion

I would venture to draw an analogy between metaheuristics and the automobile. Metaheuristics are methods that can help many engineers in many fields. In the field of logistics, where the studied systems are complex, where problems are not defined with certainty, where decisions are based on many factors that not always can be modeled, the search for optimal solutions does not always make great sense. Very often, the implementation of a simple metaheuristic will amply suffice. Such metaheuristics are relatively easy to implement and we already have seen that they are quite effective. It is the car that you and I take to go to work or to go on holidays. Robust, reliable, it meets the essential needs of everyone.

And then there is the motorsport world. In the mad race of technology; the search for the moment that will make all the difference is always on. It is the academic world in all its glory. Operational researchers who imagine new resolution methods, new neighborhoods and algorithmic tricks continue in their quest for the last percentage gains. The academic is to the engineer or to the manufacturer what the sports car is to the car. It allows developing methods that are increasingly reliable, increasingly reusable and increasingly accessible.

It is in this spirit of making metaheuristics available that I conceived this book. The first part is for all those wishing to explore the world of metaheuristics and combinatorial optimization. It provides easy access to these methods and allows engineering apprentices or students to use it for their research projects. The second part is directed to a public more familiar with this type of methods. It will provide many research or reflection tips for PhD students. The last part is addressed equally to manufacturers, who must define their needs and researchers who must interpret such needs and guide future research.

I have tried throughout this book to defend the thesis that to properly meet the challenges of logistics systems, methods must unite to combine forces. Metaheuristics are fabulous methods that still make us wonder, even after years of experience, how and why they work so well. However, they do not have all the answers for all the problems. No metaheuristic is superior to another. No optimization method is superior to another. All of them have a role to play.

When I was writing this book, I had the opportunity to immerse myself in old papers, from the 1960s or 1970s, and I did it with great pleasure. I realized that the researchers of the time, still with few technological resources, often found answers in mathematical properties that helped them to move forward. The conclusion that I have drawn is that very often salvation is found in the culture, and it is with those words that I wish to conclude.

Bibliography

[ABD 04] ABDELMAGUID T.F., NASSEF A.O., KAMAL B.A. *et al.*, "A hybrid GA/heuristic approach to the simultaneous scheduling of machines and automated guided vehicles", *International Journal of Production Research*, vol. 42, no. 2, pp. 267–281, 2004.

[ABO 11] ABO-HAMAD W., ARISHA A., "Simulation-optimisation methods in supply chain applications: a review", *The Irish Journal of Management*, vol. 30, no. 2, pp. 95–124, 2011.

[ADU 15] ADULYASAK Y., CORDEAUET J.F., JANS R., "The production routing problem: a review of formulations and solution algorithms", *Computers & Operations Research*, vol. 55, pp. 141–152, 2015.

[ALM 09] ALMEDER C., PREUSSER M., HARTL R.F., "Simulation and optimization of supply chains: alternative or complementary approaches?", *OR Spectrum*, vol. 31, no. 1, pp. 95–119, 2009.

[AND 10] ANDERSSON H., HOFF A., CHRISTIANSEN M. *et al.*, "Industrial aspects and literature survey: combined inventory management and routing", *Computers & Operations Research*, vol. 37, no. 9, pp. 1515–1536, 2010.

[ARC 07] ARCHETTI C., BERTAZZI L., LAPORTEET G. *et al.*, "A branch-and-cut algorithm for a vendor-managed inventory-routing problem", *Transportation Science*, vol. 41, no. 3, pp. 382–391, 2007.

[ARC 12] ARCHETTI C., BERTAZZI L., HERTZ A. *et al.*, "A hybrid heuristic for an inventory routing problem", *INFORMS Journal on Computing*, vol. 24, no. 1, pp. 101–116, 2012.

[BEL 83] BELL W.J., DALBERTO L.M., FISHER M.L. *et al.*, "Improving the distribution of industrial gases with an on-line computerized routing and scheduling optimizer", *Interfaces*, vol. 13, no. 6, pp. 4–23, 1983.

[BIL 95] BILGE Ü., ULUSOY G., "A time window approach to simultaneous scheduling of machines and material handling system in an FMS", *Operations Research*, vol. 43, no. 6, pp. 1058–1070, 1995.

[BIX 99] BIXBY R., CHVÁTALET V., COOK W., *Finding Tours in the TSP*, Rheinische Friedrich-Wilhelms-Universität Bonn, 1999.

[BLU 03] BLUM C., ROLI A., "Metaheuristics in combinatorial optimization: overview and conceptual comparison", *ACM Computing Surveys*, vol. 35, pp. 268–308, 2003.

[BLU 11] BLUM C., PUCHINGER J., RAIDLET G. *et al.*, "Hybrid metaheuristics in combinatorial optimization: a survey", *Applied Soft Computing*, vol. 11, pp. 4135–4151, 2011.

[CAM 70] CAMPBELL H.G., DUDEK R.A., SMITH M.L., "A heuristic algorithm for the n job, m machine sequencing problem", *Management Science*, vol. 16, no. 10, pp. 630–637, 1970.

[CAM 04] CAMPBELL A.M., SAVELSBERGH M.W.P., "A decomposition approach for the inventory-routing problem", *Transportation Science*, vol. 38, no. 4, pp. 488–502, 2004.

[CHA 11] CHAUDHRY I.A., MAHMOOD S., SHAMI M., "Simultaneous scheduling of machines and automated guided vehicles in flexible manufacturing systems using genetic algorithms", *Journal of Central South University of Technology*, vol. 18, no. 5, pp. 1473–1486, 2011.

[CHR 77] CHRISTOFIDES N., Worst-case analysis of a new heuristic for the travelling salesman problem, Report 388, Carnegie-Mellon University, Pittsburgh, 1977.

[CLE 04] CLERC M., "Discrete particle swarm optimization, illustrated by the traveling salesman problem" *New Optimization Techniques in Engineering*, Springer Berlin Heidelberg, pp. 219–239, 2004.

[COE 13] COELHO L.C., CORDEAUET J.F., LAPORTE G., "Thirty years of inventory routing", *Transportation Science*, vol. 48, no. 1, pp. 1–19, 2013.

[COL 91] COLORNI A., DORIGO M., MANIEZZO V., "Distributed optimization by ant colonies", *1st European Conference on Artificial Life*, Paris, pp. 134–142, 1991.

[COO 08] COOREN Y., CLERC M., SIARRY P., "Initialization and displacement of the particles in TRIBES, a parameter-free particle swarm optimization algorithm", *Adaptive and Multilevel Metaheuristics*, Springer Berlin Heidelberg, pp. 199–219, 2008.

[CUD 15] CUDA R., GUASTAROBA G., SPERANZA M.G., "A survey on two-echelon routing problems", *Computers & Operations Research*, vol. 55, pp. 185–199, 2015.

[DAG 98] DA GAMA F.S., CAPTIVO M.E., "A heuristic approach for the discrete dynamic location problem", *Location Science*, vol. 6, pp. 211–223, 1998.

[DAN 90] DANTZIG G.B., *Origins of the Simplex Method*, ACM Digital Library, pp. 141–151, 1990.

[DER 02] DEROUSSI L., Heuristiques, métaheuristiques et systèmes de voisinage: application à des problèmes théoriques et industriels de type TSP et ordonnancement, PhD Thesis, University Blaise Pascal, Clermont-Ferrand, 2002.

[DER 05] DEROUSSI L., GOURGAND M., NORRE S., "An efficient PSO for combinatorial optimization", *International Conference on Industrial Engineering and Systems Management (IESM)*, Marrakech, Morocco, 2005.

[DER 06] DEROUSSI L., NORREET S.M., GOURGAND, New effective neighborhoods for the permutation flow shop problem, Research report LIMOS RR-06-09, 2006.

[DER 08] DEROUSSI L., GOURGAND M., TCHERNEV N., "A simple metaheuristic approach to the simultaneous scheduling of machines and automated guided vehicles", *International Journal of Production Research*, vol. 46, no. 8, pp. 2143–2164, 2008.

[DER 12] DERBEL H., JARBOUI B., HANAFI S. *et al.*, "Genetic algorithm with iterated local search for solving a location-routing problem", *Expert Systems with Applications*, vol. 39, no. 3, pp. 2865–2871, 2012.

[DER 13] DEROUSSI L., GOURGAND M., "A scheduling approach for the design of flexible manufacturing systems", in SIARRY P. (ed.), *Heuristics: Theory and Applications*, Nova Science Publishers, pp. 223–244, 2013.

[DER 14] DEROUSSI L., GRANGEON N., NORRE S., "Techniques d'hybridation à base de métaheuristiques pour optimiser des systèmes logistiques", *Métaheuristiques*, Eyrolles, pp. 363–386, 2014.

[DES 96] DESAI R., PATIL R., "SALO: combining simulated annealing and local optimization for efficient global optimization", *Proceedings of the 9th Florida AI Research Symposium (FLAIRS)*, pp. 233–237, 1996.

[DIM 00] DIMACS TSP CHALLENGE, Library of instances for the TSP, available at http://dimacs.rutgers.edu/Challenges/TSP/, 2000.

[DIM 03] DUMITRESCU I., STÜTZLE T., "Combinations of local search and exact algorithms", *Applications of Evolutionary Computing*, Springer Berlin Heidelberg, pp. 211–223, 2003.

[DOR 97] DORIGO M., GAMBARDELLA L.M., "Ant colony system: a cooperative learning approach to the traveling salesman problem", *IEEE Transactions on Evolutionary Computation*, vol. 1, no. 1, pp. 53–66, 1997.

[DOU 13] DOULABI S.H.H., SEIFI A., "Lower and upper bounds for location-arc routing problems with vehicle capacity constraints", *European Journal of Operational Research*, vol. 224, no. 1, pp. 189–208, 2013.

[DRE 97] DREXL A., KIMMS A., "Lot sizing and scheduling–survey and extensions", *European Journal of Operational Research*, vol. 99, no. 2, pp. 221–235, 1997.

[DRE 15] DREXL M., SCHNEIDER M., "A survey of variants and extensions of the location-routing problem", *European Journal of Operational Research*, vol. 241, pp. 283–308, 2015.

[DRI 07] DRIRA A., PIERREVALET H., HAJRI-GABOUJ S., "Facility layout problems: a survey", *Annual Reviews in Control*, vol. 31, no. 2, pp. 255–267, 2007.

[DUH 11] DUHAMEL C., LACOMME P., PRODHON C., "Efficient frameworks for greedy split and new depth first search split procedures for routing problems", *Computers & Operations Research*, vol. 38, no. 4, pp. 723–739, 2011.

[EBE 95] EBERHART R.C., KENNEDY J., "A new optimizer using particle swarm theory", *Proceedings of the 6th International Symposium on Micro Machine and Human Science*, vol. 1, pp. 39–43, 1995.

[EDM 65] EDMONDS J., "Paths, trees, and flowers", *Canadian Journal of Mathematics*, vol. 17, no. 3, pp. 449–467, 1965.

[FEO 95] FEO T.A., RESENDE M.G., "Greedy randomized adaptive search procedures", *Journal of Global Optimization*, vol. 6, no. 2, pp. 109–133, 1995.

[FLE 93] FLEURY G., Méthodes stochastiques et déterministes pour les problèmes NP-difficiles, PhD Thesis, University Blaise Pascal, Clermont-Ferrand, 1993.

[FLE 02] FLESZAR K., HINDI K.S., "New heuristics for one-dimensional bin-packing", *Computers & Operations Research*, vol. 29, no. 7, pp. 821–839, 2002.

[FOR 61] FORRESTER J.W., *Industrial Dynamics*, MIT Press, Cambridge, MA, 1961.

[FRE 95] FREDMAN M.L., JOHNSON D.S., MCGEOCH L.A. *et al.*, "Data structures for traveling salesmen", *Journal of Algorithms*, vol. 18, no. 3, pp. 432–479, 1995.

[FRE 96] FREISLEBEN B., MERZ P., "A genetic local search algorithm for solving symmetric and asymmetric traveling salesman problems", *Evolutionary Computation, Proceedings of IEEE International Conference on*, pp. 616–621, 1996.

[GAM 05] GAMBOA D., REGO C., GLOVER F., "Data structures and ejection chains for solving large-scale traveling salesman problems", *European Journal of Operational Research*, vol. 160, no. 1, pp. 154–171, 2005.

[GAN 95] GANESHAN R., HARRISON T.P., An introduction to supply chain management, Department of Management Science and Information Systems, Penn State University, 1995.

[GLO 92] GLOVER F., "New ejection chain and alternating path methods for traveling salesman problems", *Computer Science and Operations Research*, pp. 449–509, 1992.

[GOL 89] GOLBERG D.E., *Genetic Algorithms in Search, Optimization, and Machine Learning*, Addison Wesley, 1989.

[HAJ 88] HAJEK B., "Cooling schedules for optimal annealing", *Mathematics of Operations Research*, vol. 13, pp. 311–329, 1988.

[HEL 00] HELSGAUN K., "An effective implementation of the Lin-Kernighan traveling salesman heuristic", *European Journal of Operational Research*, vol. 126, no. 1, pp. 106–130, 2000.

[HOL 75] HOLLAND J.H., *Adaptation in Natural and Artificial Systems: an Introductory Analysis with Applications to Biology, Control, and Artificial Intelligence*, University Michigan Press, 1975.

[JOH 54] JOHNSON S.M., "Optimal two- and three-stage production schedules with setup times included", *Naval Res. Log. Quart. I*, pp. 61–68, 1954.

[JOU 09] JOURDAN L., BASSEURET M., TALBI E.G., "Hybridizing exact methods and metaheuristics: a taxonomy", *European Journal of Operational Research*, vol. 199, no. 3, pp. 620–629, 2009.

[KAR 84] KARMARKAR N., A new polynomial-time algorithm for linear programming, *Proceedings of the Sixteenth Annual ACM Symposium on Theory of Computing*, ACM, pp. 302–311, 1984.

[KIR 83] KIRKPATRICK S., VECCHI M.P., "Optimization by simulated annealing", *Science*, vol. 220, pp. 671–680, 1983.

[KOO 57] KOOPMANS T.C., BECKMAN M., "Assignment problems and the location of economic activities", *Econometric*, vol. 25, pp. 53–76, 1957.

[KOU 06] KOUVELIS P., CHAMBERS C., WANG, "Supply chain management research and production and operations management: review, trends, and opportunities", *Production and Operations Management*, vol. 15, no. 3, pp. 449–469, 2006.

[KRU 56] KRUSKAL J.B., "On the shortest spanning subtree of a graph and the traveling salesman problem", *Proceedings of the American Mathematical Society*, vol. 7, pp. 48–50, 1956.

[KUH 55] KUHN H.W., "The Hungarian method for the assignment problem", *Naval Research Logistics Quarterly*, vol. 2, pp. 83–97, 1955.

[LAC 13] LACOMME P., LARABI M., TCHERNEV N., "Job-shop based framework for simultaneous scheduling of machines and automated guided vehicles", *International Journal of Production Economics*, vol. 143, no. 1, pp. 24–34, 2013.

[LEA 06] LE-ANH T., DE KOSTER M.B.M., "A review of design and control of automated guided vehicle systems", *European Journal of Operational Research*, vol. 171, no. 1, pp. 1–23, 2006.

[LEM 08] LEMOINE D., Modèles génériques et méthodes de résolution pour la planification tactique mono-site et multi-site, PhD Thesis, University Blaise Pascal, France, 2008.

[LEN 77] LENSTRA J.K., KANET A.R., BRUCKER P., "Complexity of machine scheduling problems", *Annals of Discrete Mathematics*, vol. 1, pp. 343–362, 1977.

[LIN 73] LIN S., KERNIGHAN B.W., "An effective heuristic algorithm for the traveling-salesman problem", *Operations Research*, vol. 21, no. 2, pp. 498–516, 1973.

[LOU 01] LOURENÇO H., Supply chain management: an opportunity for metaheuristics, UPF Economics and Business Working Paper 538, 2001.

[LOU 03] LOURENÇO H., MARTIN O.C., STÜTZLE T., *Iterated Local Search*, Springer, 2003.

[MAN 60] MANNE A.S., "On the job-shop scheduling problem", *Operations Research*, vol. 8, no. 2, pp. 219–223, 1960.

[MAR 92] MARTIN O., OTTO S.W., FELTEN E.W., "Large-step Markov chains for the TSP incorporating local search heuristics", *Operations Research Letters*, vol. 11, no. 4, pp. 219–224, 1992.

[MAR 96] MARTIN O., OTTO S.W., "Combining simulated annealing with local search heuristic", *Annals of Operations Letters*, vol. 63, pp. 57–75, 1996.

[MIR 06] MIRAGLIOTTA G., "Layers and mechanisms: a new taxonomy for the bullwhip effect", *International Journal of Production Economics*, vol. 104, no. 2, pp. 365–381, 2006.

[MJI 14] MJIRDA A., JARBOUI B., MACEDO R. *et al.*, "A two phase variable neighborhood search for the multi-product inventory routing problem", *Computers & Operations Research*, vol. 52, pp. 291–299, 2014.

[MLA 97] MLADENOVIC N., HANSEN P., "Variable neighborhood search", *Computers & Operations Research*, vol. 24, no. 11, pp. 1097–1100, 1997.

[MOI 11] MOIN N.H., SALHI S., AZIZ N.A.B., "An efficient hybrid genetic algorithm for the multi-product multi-period inventory routing problem", *International Journal of Production Economics*, vol. 133, no. 1, pp. 334–343, 2011.

[MOS 89] MOSCATO P., On evolution, search, optimization, genetic algorithms and martial arts: towards memetic algorithms, Caltech concurrent computation program, C3P Report826, 1989.

[MUN 57] MUNKRES J., "Algorithms for the assignment and transportation problems", *Journal of the Society for Industrial & Applied Mathematics*, vol. 5, pp. 32–38, 1957.

[NAG 07] NAGY G., SALHI S., "Location-routing: issues, models and methods", *European Journal of Operational Research*, vol. 177, no. 2, pp. 649–672, 2007.

[NAW 83] NAWAZ M., ENSCORE E.E., HAM I., "A heuristic algorithm for the m-machine, n-job flow-shop sequencing problem", *Omega*, vol. 11, no. 1, pp. 91–95, 1983.

[NOR 05] NORRE S., Heuristiques et métaheuristiques pour la résolution de problèmes d'optimisation combinatoire dans les systèmes de production, Habilitation thesis, 2005.

[OLI 82] OLIVER R.K., WEBBER M.D., "Supply-chain management: logistics catches up with strategy", *Outlook*, vol. 5, no. 1, pp. 42–47, 1982.

[ORL 75] ORLICKY J., "MRP: material requirements planning", *The New Way of Life in Production and Inventory Management*, McGraw Hill, 1975.

[OSM 96] OSMAN I.H., LAPORTE G., "Metaheuristics: a bibliography", *Annals of Operations Research*, vol. 63, pp. 513–623, 1996.

[PRI 57] PRIM R.C., "Shortest connection networks and some generalizations", *Bell System Technical Journal*, vol. 36, pp. 1389–1401, 1957.

[PRI 07] PRINS C., PRODHON C., RUIZ A. *et al.*, "Solving the capacitated location-routing problem by a cooperative Lagrangean relaxation granular Tabu search heuristic", *Transportation Science*, vol. 41, no. 4, pp. 470–483, 2007.

[PRO 14] PRODHON C., PRINS C., "A survey of recent research on location-routing problems", *European Journal of Operational Research*, vol. 238, pp. 1–17, 2014.

[PUC 05] PUCHINGER J., RAIDL G.R., *Combining Metaheuristics and Exact Algorithms in Combinatorial Optimization: a Survey and Classification*, Springer Berlin Heidelberg, 2005.

[RED 06] REDDY B.S.P., RAO C.S.P., "A hybrid multi-objective GA for simultaneous scheduling of machines and AGVs in FMS", *The International Journal of Advanced Manufacturing Technology*, vol. 31, pp. 602–613, 2006.

[REG 98] REGO C., "Relaxed tours and path ejections for the traveling salesman problem" *European Journal of Operational Research*, vol. 106, no. 2, pp. 522–538, 1998.

[REI 91] REINELT G., "TSPLIB–a traveling salesman problem library", *Orsa Journal on Computing*, vol. 3, no. 4, pp. 376–384, 1991.

[REI 94] REINELT G., *The Traveling-Salesman: Computational Solutions for TSP Applications*, Springer, 1994.

[ROS 77] ROSENKRANTZ D.J., STEARNS R.E., LEWIS P.M. II, "An analysis of several heuristics for the traveling salesman problem", *SIAM Journal on Computing*, vol. 6, no. 3, pp. 563–581, 1977.

[SIM 03] SIMCHI-LEVI D., KAMINSKYET P., SIMCHI-LEVI E., *Designing and Managing the Supply Chain: Concepts, Strategies, and Case Studies*, McGraw-Hill, 2003.

[STO 97] STORN R., PRICE K., "Differential evolution–a simple and efficient heuristic for global optimization over continuous spaces", *Journal of Global Optimization*, vol. 11, no. 4, pp. 341–359, 1997.

[STÜ 97] STÜTZLE T., HOOS H., "MAX-MIN ant system and local search for the traveling salesman problem", *Evolutionary Computation, IEEE International Conference on*, pp. 309–314, 1997.

[STÜ 98] STÜTZLE T., Applying iterated local search to the permutation flow shop problem, FG Intellektik, TU Darmstadt, Darmstadt, Germany, 1998.

[TAI 90] TAILLARD E., "Some efficient heuristic methods for the flow shop sequencing problem", *European Journal of Operational Research*, vol. 47, pp. 67–74, 1990.

[TAI 15] TAILLARD E., Taillard's instances, available at http://mistic.heig-vd.ch/taillard/problemes.dir/ordonnancement.dir/ordonnancement.html, 2015.

[TAL 02] TALBI E.G., "A taxonomy of hybrid metaheuristics", *Journal of Heuristics*, vol. 8, no. 5, pp. 541–564, 2002.

[TIN 13] TING C.J., CHEN C.H., "A multiple ant colony optimization algorithm for the capacitated location routing problem", *International Journal of Production Economics*, vol. 141, pp. 34–44, 2013.

[ÜLU 93] ÜLUSOY G., BILGE U., "Simultaneous scheduling of machines and automated guided vehicles", *International Journal of Production Research*, vol. 31, pp. 2857–2873, 1993.

[ÜLU 97] ÜLUSOY G., SIVRIKAYA-SERIFOGLU F., BILGE U., "A genetic algorithm approach to the simultaneous scheduling of stations and automated guided vehicles", *Computers Operations Research*, vol. 24, pp. 335–351, 1997.

[VIS 06] VIS I.F., "Survey of research in the design and control of automated guided vehicle systems", *European Journal of Operational Research*, vol. 170, no. 3, pp. 677–709, 2006.

[WAG 58] WAGNER H.M., WHITIN T.M., "A dynamic version of the economic lot size model", *Management Science*, vol. 5, pp. 89–96, 1958.

[WIG 84] WIGHT O., *Manufacturing Resource Planning: MRP II: Unlocking America's Productivity Potential*, Oliver Wight, 1984.

[WIK 91] WIKNER J., TOWILL D.R., NAIM M., "Smoothing supply chain dynamics", *International Journal of Production Economics*, vol. 22, no. 3, pp. 231–248, 1991.

[WOL 97] WOLPERT D.H., MACREADY W.G., "No free lunch theorems for optimization", *IEEE Transactions on Evolutionary Computation*, vol. 1, pp. 67–82, 1997.

Index

Other titles from

in

Computer Engineering

2016

MAGOULÈS Frédéric, ZHAO Hai-Xiang
Data Mining and Machine Learning in Building Energy Analysis

2015

BARBIER Franck, RECOUSSINE Jean-Luc
COBOL Software Modernization: From Principles to Implementation with the BLU AGE® Method

CHEN Ken
Performance Evaluation by Simulation and Analysis with Applications to Computer Networks

CLERC Maurice
Guided Randomness in Optimization (Metaheuristics Set - Volume 1)

DURAND Nicolas, GIANAZZA David, GOTTELAND Jean-Baptiste, ALLIOT Jean-Marc
Metaheuristics for Air Traffic Management (Metaheuristics Set - Volume 2)

MAGOULÈS Frédéric, ROUX François-Xavier, HOUZEAUX Guillaume
Parallel Scientific Computing

MUNEESAWANG Paisarn, YAMMEN Suchart
Visual Inspection Technology in the Hard Disk Drive Industry

2014

BOULANGER Jean-Louis
Formal Methods Applied to Industrial Complex Systems

BOULANGER Jean-Louis
Formal Methods Applied to Complex Systems: Implementation of the B Method

GARDI Frédéric, BENOIST Thierry, DARLAY Julien, ESTELLON Bertrand, MEGEL Romain
Mathematical Programming Solver based on Local Search

KRICHEN Saoussen, CHAOUACHI Jouhaina
Graph-related Optimization and Decision Support Systems

LARRIEU Nicolas, VARET Antoine
Rapid Prototyping of Software for Avionics Systems: Model-oriented Approaches for Complex Systems Certification

OUSSALAH Mourad Chabane
Software Architecture 1
Software Architecture 2

PASCHOS Vangelis Th
Combinatorial Optimization – 3-volume series, 2nd Edition
Concepts of Combinatorial Optimization – Volume 1, 2nd Edition
Problems and New Approaches – Volume 2, 2nd Edition
Applications of Combinatorial Optimization – Volume 3, 2nd Edition

QUESNEL Flavien
Scheduling of Large-scale Virtualized Infrastructures: Toward Cooperative Management

RIGO Michel
Formal Languages, Automata and Numeration Systems 1: Introduction to Combinatorics on Words
Formal Languages, Automata and Numeration Systems 2: Applications to Recognizability and Decidability

SAINT-DIZIER Patrick
Musical Rhetoric: Foundations and Annotation Schemes

TOUATI Sid, DE DINECHIN Benoit
Advanced Backend Optimization

2013

ANDRÉ Etienne, SOULAT Romain
The Inverse Method: Parametric Verification of Real-time Embedded Systems

BOULANGER Jean-Louis
Safety Management for Software-based Equipment

DELAHAYE Daniel, PUECHMOREL Stéphane
Modeling and Optimization of Air Traffic

FRANCOPOULO Gil
LMF — Lexical Markup Framework

GHÉDIRA Khaled
Constraint Satisfaction Problems

ROCHANGE Christine, UHRIG Sascha, SAINRAT Pascal
Time-Predictable Architectures

WAHBI Mohamed
Algorithms and Ordering Heuristics for Distributed Constraint Satisfaction Problems

ZELM Martin *et al.*
Enterprise Interoperability

2012

ARBOLEDA Hugo, ROYER Jean-Claude
Model-Driven and Software Product Line Engineering

BLANCHET Gérard, DUPOUY Bertrand
Computer Architecture

BOULANGER Jean-Louis
Industrial Use of Formal Methods: Formal Verification

BOULANGER Jean-Louis
Formal Method: Industrial Use from Model to the Code

CALVARY Gaëlle, DELOT Thierry, SÈDES Florence, TIGLI Jean-Yves
Computer Science and Ambient Intelligence

MAHOUT Vincent
Assembly Language Programming: ARM Cortex-M3 2.0: Organization, Innovation and Territory

MARLET Renaud
Program Specialization

SOTO Maria, SEVAUX Marc, ROSSI André, LAURENT Johann
Memory Allocation Problems in Embedded Systems: Optimization Methods

2011

BICHOT Charles-Edmond, SIARRY Patrick
Graph Partitioning

BOULANGER Jean-Louis
Static Analysis of Software: The Abstract Interpretation

CAFERRA Ricardo
Logic for Computer Science and Artificial Intelligence

HOMES Bernard
Fundamentals of Software Testing

KORDON Fabrice, HADDAD Serge, PAUTET Laurent, PETRUCCI Laure
Distributed Systems: Design and Algorithms

KORDON Fabrice, HADDAD Serge, PAUTET Laurent, PETRUCCI Laure
Models and Analysis in Distributed Systems

LORCA Xavier
Tree-based Graph Partitioning Constraint

TRUCHET Charlotte, ASSAYAG Gerard
Constraint Programming in Music

VICAT-BLANC PRIMET Pascale *et al.*
Computing Networks: From Cluster to Cloud Computing

2010

AUDIBERT Pierre
Mathematics for Informatics and Computer Science

BABAU Jean-Philippe *et al.*
Model Driven Engineering for Distributed Real-Time Embedded Systems 2009

BOULANGER Jean-Louis
Safety of Computer Architectures

MONMARCHE Nicolas *et al.*
Artificial Ants

PANETTO Hervé, BOUDJLIDA Nacer
Interoperability for Enterprise Software and Applications 2010

PASCHOS Vangelis Th
Combinatorial Optimization – 3-volume series
Concepts of Combinatorial Optimization – Volume 1
Problems and New Approaches – Volume 2
Applications of Combinatorial Optimization – Volume 3

SIGAUD Olivier *et al.*
Markov Decision Processes in Artificial Intelligence

SOLNON Christine
Ant Colony Optimization and Constraint Programming

AUBRUN Christophe, SIMON Daniel, SONG Ye-Qiong *et al.*
Co-design Approaches for Dependable Networked Control Systems

2009

FOURNIER Jean-Claude
Graph Theory and Applications

GUEDON Jeanpierre
The Mojette Transform / Theory and Applications

JARD Claude, ROUX Olivier
Communicating Embedded Systems / Software and Design

LECOUTRE Christophe
Constraint Networks / Targeting Simplicity for Techniques and Algorithms

2008

BANÂTRE Michel, MARRÓN Pedro José, OLLERO Hannibal, WOLITZ Adam
Cooperating Embedded Systems and Wireless Sensor Networks

MERZ Stephan, NAVET Nicolas
Modeling and Verification of Real-time Systems

PASCHOS Vangelis Th
Combinatorial Optimization and Theoretical Computer Science: Interfaces and Perspectives

WALDNER Jean-Baptiste
Nanocomputers and Swarm Intelligence

2007

BENHAMOU Frédéric, JUSSIEN Narendra, O'SULLIVAN Barry
Trends in Constraint Programming

JUSSIEN Narendra
A to Z of Sudoku

2006

BABAU Jean-Philippe *et al.*
From MDD Concepts to Experiments and Illustrations – DRES 2006

HABRIAS Henri, FRAPPIER Marc
Software Specification Methods

MURAT Cecile, PASCHOS Vangelis Th
Probabilistic Combinatorial Optimization on Graphs

PANETTO Hervé, BOUDJLIDA Nacer
Interoperability for Enterprise Software and Applications 2006 / IFAC-IFIP I-ESA'2006

2005

GÉRARD Sébastien *et al.*
Model Driven Engineering for Distributed Real Time Embedded Systems

PANETTO Hervé
Interoperability of Enterprise Software and Applications 2005

Lightning Source UK Ltd.
Milton Keynes UK
UKOW06n0201220617
303828UK00001B/31/P